winning

the

mind

battle

Kylie Oaks Gatewood

Harrison House

Tulsa, OK

10 9 8 7 6 5 4 3 2 1   16 17 18 19

Winning the Mind Battle
ISBN: 978-1-68031-377-2
Copyright © 2016 by Kylie Gatewood

Published by Harrison House Publishers
Tulsa, Oklahoma

Dedication

Thank you to my Jesus, for without your grace and mercy I know my life would have been over a long time ago.

Thank you to my family, those blood related and those not, who walked with me, prayed for me, contended for my life, and remained by my side all of these years.

Thank you to my husband, Jimmy, for pushing me to tell my story and the revelation the Lord implanted in me to help others.

To the members of Supernatural Life Church in Branson, MO. Thank you for believing in the call enough to see the value of this project and doing what needed to be done to carry it out.

And lastly, my precious daughters Judaea and Elliana. This book holds the story of a person you'll never have to be. If you grow up and want to read this book, remember you are so much more valuable than what others want from you. You are so loved by the Father God that he paid his best price for you. Your mommy loves you with her whole heart!

Table of Contents

1

My Story

Allow me introduce myself. My name is Kylie Gatewood, and I recently celebrated my 35th birthday. Now this might not sound like a big deal to you, but it was a BIG DEAL for me because there was a time in my life when I didn't know if I would even live past my twenties, let alone reach the age of 35!

Let's back up several years to where my story started to twist and turn. Life seemed great when I graduated from high school, but things started to change as I entered my freshman year of college. I clearly remember the day my parents dropped me off at college for the first time. As the last box was unloaded, my parents kissed me on the cheek to say goodbye and pulled out of my dorm parking lot. As I stood there, watching them drive away, I realized for the first time in my life that I did not know how to be alone.

I went from being senior class president the year before to now feeling like a nobody. Insecurities and fears I didn't even know existed began to creep into my mind. In the past, I had always made friends easily. As a matter of fact, I could walk up to a perfect stranger and strike up a conversation. But as the first weeks of my freshman year passed, the old "social" Kylie became a distant memory, and fear began to control my actions. It got to the point where I wasn't even comfortable talking to people face-to-face because I felt there was no way that anyone would like the "real" me. I began logging onto chatrooms and making connections online because there, I was able to be anyone I wanted to be. Eventually I began to search through the multitude of anonymous online faces, believing I would find a man who would validate my existence, even if it was only for one night.

A childhood experience had convinced me that sex equaled affection, approval, and ultimately, love. My walk with God started slipping rapidly as my life devolved into a series of empty sexual encounters and meaningless internet hook-ups. There was a large aching void on the inside of me, and although I tried to fill it with random strangers, my life still lacked fulfillment.

By the time my first year of college ended, I had begun to have some health issues. Truthfully, I knew what was causing those health issues. Down deep, I knew I was being disobedient! I knew I was supposed to go to Rhema Bible Training Center (RBTC), so after finishing my freshman year, I left college and went to RBTC.

I knew how to pass Bible school. I knew how to read the books, say the right words, and pass the tests. Yet the whole time I was doing all of this, I was still living like the devil!

I was going through the motions, but my heart wasn't in it because of the poor choices I was making.

I thought I had everything together. I had made it through the first 20 years of my life as a PK (preacher's kid). On the surface, I looked pretty good because I didn't party, drink, or do any of the things that preachers' kids are notorious for doing. I could quote Scripture. I could even quote whole chapters of the Bible like Ephesians chapter 1 and chapter 2. I attended class every day at RBTC and even sat under the teaching of Dr. Hagin, a prophet and amazing man of God. My pedigree was impressive — I was Billye Brim's granddaughter! Yet with all these things going for me, I was still struggling.

Upon graduation from Bible school, I felt like I was supposed to go to California to finish my undergraduate degree. So I packed up and moved to the West Coast where I finished my studies and received a degree in television production. Straight out of college, I entered the television industry and became an associate producer for the series, *Touched by an Angel*. At this point in my life, everything seemed to be back on track and going well.

But gradually, things began to change for the worse once again. Even though I was a preacher's kid and a Bible school graduate, I had become so dense spiritually that I couldn't even read my Bible. Actually, I didn't *want* to read my Bible. I was so messed up in my soul that whenever I picked up my Bible to read it, I couldn't get through one verse. Everyone around me kept telling me, "Kylie, the Bible is your answer!" But when I tried to read it, I couldn't make sense of anything. It all sounded liked gibberish to me.

You can know all kinds of things, but it's what you put into practice — what you do on a daily basis — that matters. You can know a lot of things and still be going backwards instead of moving forward. That's where I found myself. I knew a lot of things, but I had regressed to the point that I was absolutely ignorant of God's Word. And it nearly cost me my life!

The Hidden Secret

From all outward appearances, I had no reason to question God's love for me or anybody else's love for me, for that matter. My parents were married for over 30 years; the only thing that separated them was when my dad went on to be with Jesus at the age of 53. I had a great daddy. I had a great mommy. Everything was roses … except for one itty bitty issue in my life that I had covered up for over 15 years.

When I was six years old, a man who was close to my family secretly molested me repeatedly for a period of three years. He told me that if I told anyone, he would kill them and then he would kill me too. So during my childhood years, I lived in constant fear. I thought about telling my father what had happened, but then I would play the whole scenario out in my mind. *My father would kill him and wind up in prison for murder, and I would never see him again.* So I never told anyone.

Even if everything else was fine in my life, I still had this one, little hidden secret buried way down deep. The struggles that manifested when I went off to college did not begin in a single day. They were a culmination of a series of events — a series of thoughts, actually — that were leading me down a dangerous path. And it all started with one particular thought.

Thoughts are Powerful

As I grew older, I thought that I had forgiven the man who molested me, but I had actually only pushed my hurt and resentment down deep. Some days I didn't think about it, but other days, the pictures of past events would appear very vividly in my mind, and I would remember some aspect of what had happened. On those days, it was as if I was reliving some parts of the situation.

I went through junior high, high school, college, Bible school and the start of my career, still suppressing these thoughts, but then all of a sudden, this itty bitty, seemingly unrelated thought came. *Do you remember all of the choir concerts and all the ballgames your parents missed because they were in the ministry?* As I started thinking about it, resentment began to take root. I thought, *You're right! They missed more than they made.*

When those thoughts came to my mind, I didn't deal with them correctly. I didn't address the issue; I just pushed my feelings down again. As a result, the devil began having a heyday in my mind, bringing up all kinds of things from the past. I started thinking, *If they had cared about you, if they were really watching out for you and not out trying to save the world, they would have noticed that there was something going on with you as a little girl. If they were really being the parents that they were supposed to be, this heartache and pain that you've gone through for all these years would not still be bothering you now that you're 22 years old.*

If I had been truthful with myself, I'd have to acknowledge that wasn't even close to what life was really like with my parents. Both of my parents were very protective of me. I had the best parents in the whole world.

My parents weren't the issue; the secret I had kept since my childhood was the real issue. That man who molested me for all those years had planned out everything very well. He threatened me, so I lived in fear of what he might do to me or someone else if

I told anyone about his offenses. I allowed his words and actions to define love for me, but the idea of love that I had in my mind was the furthest thing from what real love is. Yet, I believed the lies the enemy was feeding me. I accepted them as truth.

As I entered into my early twenties, the pain, the agony, the anxiety, and the unforgiveness all continued to build up within me. I knew the Word of God. I knew what I should be doing to defeat the attacks of the enemy, but I wasn't doing it. Remember, it's not what you know; it's what you do. I knew what to do, but I chose to handle my problems a different way.

I wasn't staying on the offensive in my battle against the enemy, which only added to the problem. It came to the point that I just thought, *I gotta have a little bit of relief here. I'm not making it.* My own mind was tormenting me, so I started drinking to quiet some of the thoughts. I would crack open a beer on the way to work and drink it. Then as soon as I left work, I would go to the bar and have another beer. Eventually, I became a hard-core drinker, but the more I drank the more depressed I became. So I tried to lay off the alcohol, but found that the less I drank the more depressed I became. It was a no win situation. My life was a total mess!

One day, I decided to fully buy into the thoughts the enemy sent to me: *No one cares about you anyway. No one would care if you weren't here. Why don't you just kill yourself?* This led to my first suicide attempt. I tried to overdose on a bottle of pills, but to my disappointment, somebody found me. I woke up in the ER, and I was mad.

I was diagnosed with borderline personality disorder, put on medications, and started in therapy. Trust me, there aren't a lot of therapists who like to handle borderline people for many reasons. One of the main reasons being that people with borderline personality disorder take no personal responsibility for what's happening. They always think it's somebody else's fault, not their own.

With a diagnosis like that, the experts were pretty much telling me that I was going to have to deal with this issue for the rest of my life. I didn't like their diagnosis, so I rebelled. I continued to be mad and let the devil bombard my mind with his lies. This ultimately led to suicide attempt number 2. This time, I tried to cut my wrists, but I found out that I cut them the wrong way. You know, at that point, I felt like such a failure. I couldn't even kill myself successfully! I mulled this over in my mind, *What kind of failure can't even kill themselves the right way?*

Though I had given up on myself, my mother and grandmother had not. They prayed for me every day, daring to believe that I would come out of this darkness that consumed me at the time. I now know that God heard their prayers and never stopped acting on my behalf; but at the time, I was too blind to see His hand at work in my life. (Please continue to read all the way to the end of this book, as you will be blessed by the word from my mother in the chapter entitled "A Parent's Perspective.")

With two failed suicide attempts now on my record, people around me had started to say things like, "She'd kill herself successfully if she really wanted to. She's just out to get attention." If you've been dealing with suicidal issues like I was, understand that people around you who will say things like this are yielding themselves to the enemy. He uses their words to put thoughts, ideas, and suggestions in your soul to wreak havoc in your life. The

Bible tells us we don't wrestle against flesh and blood. It's not the people around you who are saying things like that to you. It is the enemy of your soul.

I was at the bottom of the bottom. I was at the lowest of the low. I had lost my job. I was living in my car. I was completely homeless. I didn't have enough money to buy a bottle of water, let alone food or anything else. That was definitely *not* where God intended for me to be! I realize that trying to encapsulate my story in just a few pages here highlights how extreme it is. Not everyone goes from a loving home to the point of being homeless, destitute, and wanting to kill themselves, but that's what happened to me. Though not everyone's story takes the same path mine has, what you need to understand is what happened to me didn't happen all of a sudden. It was a process.

I continued to listen to the lies of the devil over and over. I finally got to the point where I wanted the voices to stop! One day, I started drinking in the morning and drank all afternoon and all night. My goal was to pass out as quickly as possible. It was the only way I could think of to make the voices stop. After multiple suicide attempts, they decided that I really was a danger to myself, so they locked me up in the worst place I could ever imagine — a state mental facility with a lot of people who, like me, seriously needed help.

I remember the night my friend dropped me off at the state mental facility because I was in yet another downward spiral. The first thing the facility staff did was take off every single piece of my clothing, told me to spread, and proceeded to check every orifice of my body to make sure I didn't have anything I could use to hurt myself or others. You are never more vulnerable than when you are naked. In that moment, I thought, *My God, how far have I fallen? I'm a Rhema Bible Training Center graduate. I'm Billye Brim's granddaughter — not that anybody in this place knows or cares.* Truthfully, right then I didn't want to be known as Billye Brim's granddaughter. I wanted to be Kylie. I wanted to have my own identity. Why? Because the devil pulled out a little arrow and said, "You need your own identity," and I believed his lie.

After enduring the humiliating strip search, they took me to a huge room filled with struggling people. There was one man who walked around exhibiting two different personalities. You could choose to talk to either one of them, and they both talked to each other. I thought, *I'm not that bad ... but this is scaring the mess out of me.*

To my utter surprise and disappointment, they didn't give me a bed. They gave me a wooden chair and a blanket. About 11:00 at night, I pulled that wooden chair over into a corner and thought, *I want to get as far away from these people as I possibly can.* I sat in the corner and got mad. I was mad because I was there, and I was mad because I knew better. I began to think, *Why am I here? Who brought me to this place? What choices landed me here? Why don't I want to live? Is life really that bad?* It was a long night, to say the least.

Around 5:00 in the morning, a doctor doing his rounds made his way to my corner. After he read my chart, he looked at me and said, "Ah, let's see (tapping his clipboard with his pen). Kylie Oaks. Kylie Oaks. Kylie Oaks. That name sounds so familiar." Then after another moment of thinking, he asked, "Aren't you Billye Brim's granddaughter?" *You've got to be kidding me!* I couldn't think of a comment that would have made me more angry, but the reality was that God knew what He was doing. I couldn't outrun the plan of God, no matter what castles were built in my mind. He had His eye on me and was working on my behalf, even when I didn't know enough to see it.

But the doctor wasn't done. He continued talking, saying, "Oh, I'm a ministry partner of hers." I was so mad! Just when I thought I couldn't be more angry, the doctor said he wanted to take my case on personally. I flipped back at him in the most hateful voice I could muster, "I bet you would." In response, he simply gave me his card and left.

Bulldog Determination

No matter what anybody said to me, no matter how many scriptures people gave me, I was not at all ready to listen. That is, until I was ready for change. One day a clear thought came. Now that I look back, I know it came from my spirit. *I don't want to look at every relationship I have for the rest of my life, through the glasses of my hurts, my pains, my experiences, my habits, and my hang-ups.* Finally, I had arrived at the point where I was tired of living a defeated life and wanted to change. It took a long time to arrive at that point, but I became bulldog-determined that I was tired of living like this, and it was time for change! I didn't know how to really change, but I was determined to do it.

I still had no desire whatsoever to read the Bible. Thoughts would come to my mind that would keep me from wanting to go to God's Word: *You need to die. No one cares if you're alive or dead. What good are you doing anybody? You can't even kill yourself right. You can't do anything right. What kind of wife would you be? What kind of mother would you be? You're all used up.* It was a struggle, but I was so bulldog-determined to take control over my soul, that I began to make myself take the steps necessary to find the Word of God concerning my situation. I determined that I would say what I need to say from the Word and would refuse to be depressed when something negative happened.

God responded to my determination and said, *"I won't just remove the depression from you. I won't just remove this victim state, this hurt, this wound. I'll not just remove that sexual lust problem that you've been having. Because you have chosen to take control over your soul and keep your mind on Me, I'm going to do something huge. I'm going to make you doubly rich, doubly prosperous. I'm going to make you walk doubly in the favor of God, doubly blessed beyond measure because you keep your mind stayed on Me."*

I am living proof that God's Word works. When I took God at His Word, I went from being suicidal, living in my car with no money, to where I am now: happily married with a beautiful baby girl. We live in a four-bedroom, four-bath house, and I drive a brand new car. Why? Because I chose to take authority over my soul. God fulfilled His promise to me. Please don't think I'm bragging on myself; I'm bragging on God!

God doesn't want you to just get by so you're not thinking the devil's thoughts anymore. He wants to bless you so you can be a blessing to others. Can you see the bigger picture here? The bigger picture is not to just get out of your own personal mess that you're in right now. The bigger picture is that God wants to bless you so you can be a blessing — so you can teach somebody else how to control their soul. Say this out loud every day, several times a day, and let it take root in your heart:

I'm doubly wealthy.

I'm doubly prosperous.

I'm doubly victorious.

I'm doubly healthy.

I walk in the health of God.

I walk in the favor of God.

I walk in the blessing of God because my mind is stayed on Him.

If you're looking for some heavy revelation or a magic button you can push to change your life, you won't find it here. What God gave me was some profoundly practical wisdom that I will share with you. I will show you some hands-on keys for stopping the stuff that will lead you off course. In terms of your identity, you will be able to expose the lies of the devil that he will try to tell you to influence the way you think about who you are, what you look like, and what emotions you should have. You will also find practical, doable steps for applying the Word of God to your life so you can live victoriously!

One of the primary ways I got through my situation was by reading a little book by Doug Jones called *Mastering the Silence*. I decided that I could probably handle reading one page a day, so that's what I did. In Doug's book, I learned that the wiles (or fiery darts) of the devil are actually thoughts, ideas, and suggestions that he brings to our minds.

I remember something Dr. Hagin said while I attended Rhema: "You can't keep birds from flying over your head, but you can keep them from building a nest in your hair." What does that mean, you ask? It simply means that you can't keep the thoughts, ideas, and suggestions of the enemy from coming, but you don't have to let them control you. I don't think about committing suicide any more. I handled that business. And now I'm going to teach you how to handle yours!

Your Mind, Will, & Emotions

Proverbs 23:7 tells us that as a man thinks in his heart, so is he. This might be a familiar passage from the Bible, but have you really understood what the word "heart" is referring to? Is it referring to your soul? No. What is your heart? It's your spirit, the real you.

You could say, "As you choose from your spirit man, that's what you'll be." That's powerful and clear! As your spirit starts making the decisions concerning who you are and what you are allowed to think, rather than your soul dictating in these matters, your true identity will come forth. There is a big difference between what is in your spirit (your heart) and what is in your soul (your mind, will, and emotions).

The "Real" You

And the Lord God formed man of the dust of the ground, and breathed into his nostrils the breath of life; and man became a living soul.

Genesis 2:7

In Hebrew, the term "living soul" literally means "a speaking spirit like God." In order to illustrate this verse, let's pretend that I call on a volunteer named Lisa to come up and stand beside me in a classroom setting, and I ask the class, "Can you see Lisa?" How would you answer that question? Most everyone in the room would nod to agree that they can, in fact, see Lisa. I would then say that if the question had been a test, most of those in the classroom would have failed!

Even though Lisa is standing right there, the truth is, you cannot see Lisa! You can see the "house" that Lisa lives in—her earth suit, if you will. But you do not see the "real" Lisa.

The "real" Lisa lives on the inside of that earth suit (body). It's the same way with an astronaut who has to wear a spacesuit to live in space. The "real" Lisa is a spirit. She has a soul, which consists of her mind, will, and emotions. Her soul is distinct from her spirit. She is a spirit because, just like you and I, she is created in the likeness and image of God.

So God created man in his own image, in the image of God created he him, male and female created he them.

Genesis 1:27

John 4:24 tells us that God is a spirit. He created us as spirit beings so we can communicate and have communion with Him, spirit to spirit. But since you are a spirit being, the only way you can get around on this planet is to live in a body. You are a spirit, you have a soul, and you live in a body. There are three parts to you.

Spirit, Soul & Body

If God communicates with you spirit to spirit, how does the devil communicate with you? That may be a new thought to you, but the devil does communicate with you. How does he do it? The devil doesn't communicate with you spirit to spirit like God does. The devil can only communicate with you through your soul. That is his only access point — the only wavelength or door he can use to communicate with and attempt to control you. He uses Your mind, will, and emotions.

Let's take a look at 1 Thessalonians 5:23. This verse shows us all three parts of man. Circle these parts in your Bible. (Yes, it's okay to write in your Bible!)

And the very God of peace sanctify you wholly; and I pray God your whole spirit and soul and body be preserved blameless unto the coming of our Lord Jesus Christ.

1 Thessalonians 5:23

You have to understand that you are a spirit. You have a soul — mind, will, and emotions — and you live in a body. Say this out loud: "I am a spirit. I have a soul. I live in a body."

If you don't understand this concept, you will think you're a bad person based on the thoughts you think. Then the devil will condemn you and say things like, "Well, if you weren't a bad person, you wouldn't think those thoughts. You wouldn't be looking at that pornography. You wouldn't have trouble with anger, fear, depression, jealousy, hatred, and lust in all forms."

We've all heard condemning words like this at some point in our lives, but the devil is feeding us a pack of lies. He wants us to think that nobody else struggles in their thought life except us. He has used these tactics on all of us. That's what he does. Remember, the devil doesn't ever do anything new under the sun!

Quench the Fiery Darts

Finally, my brethren, be strong in the Lord, and in the power of his might. Put on the whole armor of God, that ye may be able to stand against the wiles of the devil. For we wrestle not against flesh and blood, but against principalities, against powers, against the rulers of the darkness of this world, against spiritual wickedness in high places. Wherefore take unto you the whole armor of God, that ye may be able to withstand in the evil day, and having done all, to stand. Stand therefore, having your loins girt about with truth, and having on the breastplate of righteousness; and your feet shod with the preparation of the gospel of peace; above all, taking the shield of faith, wherewith ye shall be able to quench all the fiery darts of the wicked.

Ephesians 6:10-16

We need to be strong in the Lord and in the power of His might. So many times we try to do it in our own strength, but it doesn't work that way. Notice that we are told that we don't wrestle with flesh and blood. That means your momma's not your problem. Your daddy's not your problem. Whoever you think is your problem for whatever reason, they are not your problem. The real enemy is the spirit behind that person you're wanting to blame — the evil spirit that convinced that person to act as they did toward you.

Look at verse 16 in the passage we just read. In your own Bible, circle the words "above all." This means that what follows these two words is much more important than anything that had just been said. Notice that above all, we are told to take the shield of faith to quench all the fiery darts of the wicked one — the devil.

Think about the lies the devil has told you: *This person doesn't love you. That person didn't love you, either. You're unlovable. You'll never find a mate. If you do find someone, you'll drive them away because you're so crazy. You're damaged goods.* These are the fiery darts — the thoughts, ideas, and suggestions — that the enemy has thrown at you that have stuck in your soul.

Sometimes these thoughts can be random. For instance, you can be driving down the road to go to a restaurant or to go home after work, and all of a sudden, a thought comes floating across your mind and you ask yourself, *Where did that come from?* You know for sure that it didn't come from God. The devil just pulls out those little arrows of his — a thought, idea, or suggestion — and *bing!* He shoots it toward your forehead. That's a fiery dart!

Now, just because you have this thought doesn't make you a bad person. Why? Because it is not your thought. So many times when I'm counseling people, they'll say, "Pastor Kylie, I'm a terrible person because I can't shake these thoughts; I keep thinking them." Then they start defining themselves by those thoughts.

For example, I had a baby recently, and while I was pregnant, I gained a lot of weight. In the process, my blood pressure skyrocketed, and I was put on bed rest. My doctor didn't want me to move. So there I was lying in bed, and the enemy came with thoughts about my dad dying of a stroke. *Look, you are gonna be just like your daddy. You're going to die. You're only 32 years old and you're already on blood pressure medicine. You're already on bed rest with this baby. You're going to die in childbirth.*

Oh, the devil came with those thoughts, just nipping away at me. Of course, I knew that I had been redeemed from all of this, but the enemy still came to me with these thoughts. Have you ever noticed that the devil never picks something that is a far off impossibility? It's always something that has an inkling of possibility in it, right? He started showing me pictures in my mind all over again of what my dad's dead body looked like in his casket. Then, I even began to visualize my own funeral! All of these imaginations were coming at my mind. I knew I had a choice to make. Was I going to let the enemy win this battle, or was I going to win?

Immediately, I began to exercise. Why? Because I realized that if my body was stronger and if I lost a little weight, my blood pressure wouldn't remain high. So I started walking and doing what I needed to do in the natural. Later when my daughter, Judaea, was born, I realized that I had done so much walking that my legs were strong. However, I had not exercised my arms, so my little seven-pound baby was making my arms sore! As my daughter grew and gained weight, it became harder and harder to handle her.

It's the same way spiritually — the strongest part of you wins. Whatever you feed gets stronger and wins. If you feed your soul, your soul wins. If you feed your spirit, your spirit wins. If you feed your body, your body is going to win. (That was my problem. I fed my body a little too much!)

When I am teaching this in a live setting, I ask everyone, "How many of you have been dealing with thoughts, ideas, and suggestions of the enemy today? Don't be ashamed to raise your hand." When I look across the room, I see every single person raise his or her hand. Be honest with yourself right now. Have you dealt with thoughts, ideas, and suggestions of the enemy today? Every one of us face this on a daily basis.

Remember, Ephesians chapter 6 says that above all, we are to take the shield of faith so we can quench all the fiery darts of the wicked one. Did this say that we can only quench or stop *some* of the fiery darts (thoughts from the enemy) that come our way? No, it says we can quench *all* of them! It is possible to quench *all* the fiery darts of the wicked one so that those crazy thoughts cannot affect your life. They will fall dead — null and void — before they go any further.

CHAPTER

3

Castles in Your Mind

A renewed mind is the devil's worst nightmare come true. Why would the devil hate it when someone has a renewed mind? Very simply, the mind is the only means he has to get to us. That's his only access point to our lives. So if we renew our minds, the devil has no access to our lives. That's really good news!

Now the question is, "How does the devil access our minds?" He accesses our minds through our thoughts. My own story specifically started with one simple thought. Let's take a look into the Word of God and I'll show you what I mean. Every person has to deal with "castles" in their minds. Not everyone's situation is as extreme as mine was, obviously, but there is no one who is exempt, no one who doesn't have to learn how to control their soul.

> **For the weapons of our warfare are not carnal, but mighty through God to the pulling down of strong holds.**
>
> **2 Corinthians 10:4**

Circle those words "strongholds." In the Greek, the word "strongholds" is a very old word with two meanings. Rick Renner has some excellent teaching on the word "strongholds," if you'd like to find it on the Internet, but for the sake of understanding, I'll give you the short version here. Both of the meanings of "strongholds" work in this situation. The meaning is described as a place like a castle or a fortress. If you are dealing with a stronghold in your mind, it's as if a lie has been in your head for so long that it's become like a castle sitting inside your head. The devil moves in and from this lofty place, he begins to dictate what you think, what you feel, and the way you see yourself.

The second definition of "strongholds" also works in this situation. The second definition is "a prison." Seemingly these definitions paint pictures of two different things. A castle is something with big walls that tries to keep things from coming in. In a prison, you're behind bars and can only see what is on the other side. You are on the inside looking out, as the prison keeps you from going out.

When a stronghold is built up in your mind, this lie creates a huge fortress from which the devil will dictate what you should think, how you should feel, and how you should interpret situations in your life. Sometimes people aren't actually doing anything wrong to you, but you're seeing their actions as all wrong. You've worn these glasses of hurt and unforgiveness for so long — the glasses of "this happened to me in my childhood," or whatever your case may be — that you see situations in life now through the lens of those past hurts, rejections, and experiences, and you are isolated with no one getting in and no one going out.

This also reminds me of the word *oppression*. The word *oppressed* in the Greek means an entity or a lie, like a wicked king or a tyrant ruling in your head. Oppression terrorizes your life. An example of this is found in the book of Acts.

How God anointed Jesus of Nazareth with the Holy Ghost and with power: who went about doing good, and healing all that were oppressed of the devil; for God was with him.

Acts 10:38

At the time, I didn't understand all this. As a girl wanting love, I decided that the only way I could find it was to have sex with whomever I could. I longed for that feeling of love, even though it wasn't really love at all. Then the thoughts started coming, *Sex equals love, so go get all you can. You don't know what love really is because your family chose the whole world and lost their daughter. Because this man did that to you, you're used goods. Who would want to be with you?* I would give myself to random people I didn't even know. I'd meet them in a bar for a one-night stand, have sex with them, and think that I was truly trying to find love. This was a castle — a stronghold — that had built itself up in my mind, and I was seeing the whole world through this.

Everything changed for the worst when I started accepting those thoughts as truth. When you listen to the lies of the enemy — those thoughts, those ideas, those suggestions — and accept them as truth, they start to affect you. Truth always lines up with God's Word. I guarantee that none of that mess was in the Word of God. None of it!

But the devil wasn't happy with me just drinking and sleeping around. His ultimate goal was to steal, kill, and destroy my life (John 10:10). Ultimately, he wanted me to either get a STD and die or just be so broken that I wanted to die. That is exactly what happened; I just wanted to die! As I gave away a piece of myself here and there, I didn't want to live anymore. The satisfaction of love that I thought I would find in the arms of somebody I hardly knew in a bedroom, wasn't doing it for me. I didn't feel loved. I felt so empty. I felt so broken. I truly just wanted to die and get it over with.

If my life is proof of nothing else, it is proof of the fact that even when things look their very worst, God does provide a way out. Let's take a look at 2 Corinthians 10:5. This verse adds more insight into how to handle these strongholds.

Cast Down Imaginations

In Genesis chapter one, God created His world by speaking it into existence. He spoke words. If we are created in God's image and likeness (and we read that we are, indeed), it stands to reason that we create our world just as our Creator did — by speaking! We create the framework of our minds, what we're allowed to think and what we're not allowed to think, by speaking. Our words are extremely important!

In 2 Corinthians 10:5, we are told to cast down imaginations. You can do this very simply by putting your hand on your head and saying, *That is not my thought. I only think thoughts of life. I do not think thoughts of death. I plead the blood of Jesus over my mind, in Jesus' name.* The enemy cannot cross the blood of Jesus applied to your life and situation!

> **Casting down imaginations, and every high thing that exalteth itself against the knowledge of God, and bringing into captivity every thought to the obedience of Christ.**
>
> **2 Corinthians 10:5**

The word "imaginations" in the Greek, is the word *logismos*. This is where we get our word *logical*. There are two types of imaginations. There is the logical imagination and there is an illogical one.

A great example of a logical imagination is when the Holy Spirit tells you to give a certain amount of money in the offering. The logical imagination says, *I can't give that much in the offering because I wouldn't be able to pay this back and I wouldn't be able to do that.* Just like that, you reason yourself out of what the Holy Spirit tells you to do. Why? It's logical. Right? Logical imaginations are the hardest ones to overcome. Not that this is impossible to overcome them; they are just harder to do because they make sense.

An example of an illogical imagination is when the devil comes and lies to you, like he does to a person with an eating disorder. This person is extremely skinny, yet feels like she is overweight. When she looks in the mirror, she sees a 200-pound reflection, but anybody else looking at her can see that she is nothing more than skin and bones. The devil took something that was completely illogical and set up a stronghold in her mind, will, and emotions. He fed her a lie and she chose to accept it.

Handle Your Thoughts

The shield of faith plays an important part in helping you ward off those imaginations from the enemy. How do you release your faith? With your mouth, through the words you say. This is the answer to everything. You must learn that once you accept a lie as truth, it will become one of your beliefs. Once it becomes a belief, you will start acting like it's true. Everything you do starts with a thought. Thoughts can be categorized into two groups: 1) thoughts of life and 2) thoughts of death. Thoughts are not always extreme like *kill yourself,* but deadly thoughts can be anything that is anti-God, anti-anointing, anti-Christ, or anti-life.

You can be free from the lies that the devil sends to steal, kill, and destroy. It is vitally important that you deal with those thoughts, ideas, and suggestions quickly and in line with the Word of God. Your thinking determines your emotions. Your emotions determine your decisions. Your decisions determine your actions. Your actions determine your habits. Your habits determine your character.

I didn't handle my thoughts or emotions. I didn't handle my hatred, anger, or unforgiveness. And because I didn't handle them, these things affected my character. I had to learn to deal with all of these things in order to have victory over them. I'm not trying to preach to you or make you feel bad. I've been where you are. If you've been struggling, I want you to know you're not alone. I've got good news for you! You can look at me and my life now and know that there is hope. I am 35 years old and have been totally free from all that junk for more than 10 years. I no longer have thoughts about committing suicide. It never crosses my mind. I don't have thoughts about being used up or being unlovable. Why? Because perfect love casts out fear! God is love!

There is no fear in love; but perfect love casts out fear.

1 John 4:18

I don't care how used up you feel, the perfect love of God, the grace of God, and the mercy of God drive away all the hurt and pain and fear. God is truly perfect in all of His ways! You may be living like the devil like I did, but God sees you through grace. God sees you through the blood of Jesus, and you are perfect in all of your ways! Now, it's time to learn.

4

You Can Change

The key to change in your life is simple. Opening your mouth is the shield of faith. If you want to change, pull up that shield of faith, and say to the devil, "Not here, bad boy. Not here! Freedom reigns in this place, in Jesus' name!"

When you learn how to deal with the devil and go on the offensive instead of the defensive, the devil will not be able to find any place in your life. You can't stop him from trying, but his arrows will slide right off of you without impact.

My husband, Jimmy, and I have been married for over three years. We have never — I'm not lying to you — never raised our voices to one another. Do we ever disagree? Oh, absolutely! I'm a woman; he's a man! But you know, our disagreements just don't have to be explosive. I can say to him, "Now honey, this is the way I see it. "And he'll say, "No, this is the way I see it." Then we meet in the middle and work it out.

I am determined that my daughter will never hear us fight. But if you let the devil keep a foothold in your life — in your soul, in your mind — you will find that you take every single little thing that your mate does and turn it into something that offends you. This is not how you bring change into your life! I may sound rough, but I've lived, and I overcame this mess. I have learned that you have to be bulldog-determined to get rid of all the mess in your life if you want freedom in your home, if you want freedom in your life, and if you want freedom in your marriage!

Peace .... Shalom

Thou wilt keep him in perfect peace, whose mind is stayed on thee: because he trusteth in thee.

Isaiah 26:3

The word "Thou" in this verse is referring to the Father. Read that verse again. Underline in your Bible the words "perfect peace." What is the qualifier to walking in perfect peace? Having your mind stayed on God because you trust in Him.

The word "perfect" in Hebrew is the word *shalom,* and it means nothing missing, nothing broken. It's not just a word of greeting like saying, "Hey!" It's a blessing Jewish people say every time they greet each other with the word *shalom.* They are declaring over each other, "Whatever is missing in your life, I proclaim that it's no longer missing. Whatever is broken in your life, I proclaim that it's no longer broken."

It's interesting to learn that the word translated "peace" is also the word *shalom.* So in the Hebrew, this verse would say, *"Thou wilt keep him in shalom shalom whose mind is stayed on You."* When God uses a word two times in a row He is in "get your attention" and "multiplication" mode. The word *shalom* in its root also means salvation. But it doesn't just mean salvation for your soul, it's also talking about health, prosperity, wealth, and goodness. It means all of these good things. Actually, this verse could be broken down like this: *I will make you doubly peaceful. I'll make you doubly prosperous. I'll make you doubly victorious, whose mind is stayed on Me.* That is shouting ground for you right here! That is the blessing part!

In Hebrew, the word "stayed" paints a word picture. Have you ever built a house or watched a house being built? It starts with some little old two-by-fours. They're just small timbers, but they're going to frame the whole house. The word "stayed" means framed. You can think of it this way: "I will keep you in shalom shalom (perfect peace — nothing missing, nothing broken) and doubly wealthy, doubly healthy, doubly wise, if your mind has a frame and you tell your mind what you are allowing it to think and what you are not allowing it to think."

For example, when I used to do a lot of teaching in children's church and classes, we made this stuff called *gack*. Are you familiar with gack? It's made out of Borax, Elmer's Glue, and water. It's similar to slime. The weird thing about it is that when you squeeze it, it feels hard. But if you just put gack in your hand and allow gravity to do its thing, the gack becomes a soft slime that oozes through your fingers. This perfectly illustrates what happens to your mind when you do not keep it in the confines of a framework. If you do not dictate what your mind is allowed to think and what it is not allowed to think, it will run like gack does through your fingers.

Thoughts, ideas, and suggestions will come, and you'll think, *I guess I'm not a good Christian.* But that is not coming from you; it's not your thought. And God had nothing to do with it either. The devil brings those thoughts. He does what he does, as he tries to use his wiles against you. You can't completely stop the devil from doing what he tries to do because you live on this planet. But the fact of the matter is, his fiery darts don't have to torment you.

Anger, stress, jealousy, and even some trust issues all start with an itty bitty thought. With anger specifically, you're just kind of ticked off at a situation. It starts out pretty small. For example, I love to cook. I do it a lot. It's fun for me. Have you ever whisked fresh cream with a wire whisk, not with your handy dandy KitchenAid, but with a plain old hand whisk? You add a little sugar to that cream, and you just start whisking away. Now at first, the cream in the bowl is relatively smooth; it has no ripples. But the minute a little agitation comes to it, what happens? A few bubbles start to form, and it gets a little bubbly on the top. Then the more you whisk and the more effort that goes into the cream, it starts to stiffen up and grow in volume. Eventually when you whisk it long enough, you can make a sharp peak with the cream, and it will stay in that position.

Think of this image of whipped cream when you think of anger. You have to stop your thoughts before they harden. Say your confessions. Tell your soul what it is allowed to think when you see just a couple of bubbles of anger. If you can be strong enough to stop when it's just a couple of bubbles, it will not ruin your life or cut someone with its sharp peak once it grows and hardens.

Husbands and wives, you know when something is ticking you off. Ladies, when your husband has once again not picked up his underwear or once again has not put down the toilet seat, you will probably get upset with him. But whatever it is that ticks you off a little, at that point when it's just a couple of bubbles, choose to manage how you respond.

Learn how to dictate what your soul is allowed to do. How should you handle the things that come your way? What do you do first? First of all, you have to identify the enemy and that's the devil, not your husband, wife, kids, or whomever. Second, you need to judge your thought. How do you judge it? You need to realize that the thought of you getting angry is not in line with the Word of God. So, judge that thought. If it is not a Word thought—a life thought—then it is a death thought.

Take Inventory of Your Thoughts

I'll share my experience of how I got free from those thoughts, which had tormented me since childhood. It's not some heavy duty revelation; it's actually so practical that anyone can do it! The first thing I had to do was to identify the enemy. You'd think that would be pretty easy to do since the answer is always the same. The devil is our enemy. But in my case, I had to realize that my brain wasn't the enemy. The enemy was the devil. Once I got that straight, I began to understand his tactics: thoughts, ideas, and suggestions.

When I was in the middle of all that, I did not trust myself to just think. It sounds weird, but I really didn't. So this is what I had to do. I had to get down to the raw nitty-gritty and inventory every thought I had. I had to think about what I was thinking about. I couldn't let my mind just go rampant.

I had to start judging every thought and putting it into one of two piles: thoughts of life or thoughts of death. For example, if the thought came to me: *No one loves you Kylie Oaks,* I would have to analyze that thought. Okay, that is not a thought of life. That thought went into the pile of death thoughts. Then a thought might come such as, *I need to use the washroom.* I would judge it. Yes, that's a good and needful thing, so that thought went into the pile of life thoughts. It started out that elementary where I had to take every thought into captivity and judge which pile it went into.

Whenever there was a death thought — not so specific as, *You deserve to die,* but death as in being anti-life or anti-God — I had to recognize it for what it was and deal with it accordingly. This is the key to your victory right now. If you do this, I promise, you will get free. It is not about doing it one time; this practice is the sum total of all its parts. When I first started doing this, I did it upwards of 200 times a day. I'm not kidding you!

I would say these things out loud in the most embarrassing places on the planet, like the peanut butter aisle in Wal-Mart. A death thought would come to me, and I'd be whispering, *No, not now!* But I knew that if I didn't keep a leg up on the devil, he would keep a leg up on me. So I would stop there in the store or wherever I was and put my hand on my head as a point of contact and say, "In the name of Jesus, that is not my thought."

What was I doing? First of all, I was telling that thought it did not belong to me, and I was rejecting the thought of the enemy. Then I would say, "In the name of Jesus, I plead the blood of Jesus over my mind. I only think thoughts of life. I do not think thoughts of death. That is not my thought. I refuse that thought. I don't have issues about that anymore." After doing that, I would go on.

Once I got a little stronger in this, I would insert a bit of Scripture that talks about life. I would find a scripture that pertained to the situation that I was dealing with at the time. If I was dealing with my self-esteem, I would insert a scripture about who I was in Christ Jesus.

I started out with the bare basics in Scripture and went from speaking these things to myself 200 times or more a day to about 150, then to about 100. I kept going; I would not give up until I was the master of my mind. It came down to 25 times a day and fewer. Then finally one day, all of a sudden it seemed like, I woke up and realized that for the whole day before, I had not thought about dying — not one single time!

When I was dealing with anger issues and that anger would start bubbling up inside of me, I would lay my hand on my head and say, "In the name of Jesus, I plead the blood of Jesus over my mind. I only think thoughts of life. I do not think thoughts of death. I do not have an anger issue." I started calling those things that be not as though they were (Romans 4:17). I confessed, "I don't have anger issues anymore." Now you might ask, "Isn't that lying?" No! It's going back to who you truly are. I knew these things were true because I'm a child of God. I've been made in the image of God.

It's important to remember that you are not responsible for anyone else's behavior. You can't force your husband to pick up his dirty underwear. Ladies, nagging doesn't work! Ever! But a lot of times what happens in a relationship when you work to take control your thoughts and emotions is that your husband sees that you're a person he wants to live with and that you're peaceable, walking in the fruit of the Spirit. Then he starts to want to please you in a way he never has before.

When your husband sees that there's been a real change in you, he will begin to change, too, whether he knows it or not. But realize that you're not reading this book in order to change other people. You're here to change yourself and how you respond to things. It's amazing how the rest of your world falls into alignment once you've handled your own business. I'm not saying it's all roses and you're never going to have another problem with the underwear or the toilet seat or whatever causes you to become angry or agitated. But you can come to the place where you just really don't even care. All of a sudden, you start putting his dirty underwear in the hamper yourself or putting the toilet seat down, because it just doesn't bother you like it used to.

> **Whether therefore ye eat, or drink, or whatsoever ye do, do all to the glory of God. Give none offence, neither to the Jews, nor to the Gentiles, nor to the church of God.**
>
> **1 Corinthians 10:31-32**

Notice that it says, "Do all." This verse is saying that whatever you do, whether it's eating or drinking or whatsoever you do, do it *all* to the ... what? Do it all to the glory of God. That means everything! Even cleaning up after a poopy diaper. Putting the toilet seat down. Whatever you hate doing, if you change your mindset and change your perception, everything will change.

After my daughter was born, my mother said to me, "Kylie, you have a child now. Whatever you do with her, do it to the glory of God. Say, 'I pick up this toy to the glory of God. I make this bed to the glory of God. I do her hair to the glory of God.'" Mom's advice was right on, and it gave me a higher perspective. When my daughter was at the stage when she wanted to nurse every two hours in the middle of the night, I had to decide if I would get really frustrated about it, or if I would view the situation from a higher place. The higher perspective said, "I'm anointed to be a mother. I thank God that I am able to nurse my child. There are many mothers who want to and are not able to do it. This may be an inconvenience now, but it's just a season. Soon there'll be a new season where she'll sleep through the night, and I won't have to do this every-two-hour thing again."

What happened? I changed my perception of the situation. You can do that too, with everything in your life. My mom and dad were married for 30 years, yet my dad never did get quite trained to put his underwear into the bin like he was supposed to do. But do you know what my mother did? She came up into that higher place. She changed her perception of the underwear situation. She said, "Whatever I do, whether I eat or drink or whatever I do, I'm going to do it to Your glory, God. I pick up these undies to the glory of God."

Whatever you do, even if it's your job that you don't really love so much, if you choose to change your perspective and do it to the glory of God, there'll be a blessing in it for you. My dad may have had a problem putting underwear in the hamper, but he did so many more things that a lot of men didn't do. It's about looking at the big picture; it's pulling back and changing that narrow perception that you have about every situation in your life. Whatever you eat, whatever you drink, whatever you do, do all to the glory of God.

CHAPTER

5

Forgiveness: What It Is & How to Do It

Forgiveness is an extremely important part of both getting free and staying free. In fact, you won't be free without forgiving.

And lead us not into temptation, but deliver us from evil: for thine is the kingdom, and the power, and the glory, for ever. Amen. For if ye forgive men their trespasses, your heavenly Father will also forgive you.

Matthew 6:13-14

In most Bibles, these words are in red. That means Jesus is talking. Forgiveness is not always cute; it's not always pretty. But these are the words of the Savior. That means we can do it. In verse 14, underline the word "if." *If* you forgive men, your heavenly Father will also forgive you.

I now realize there are a lot of things that I thought were forgiveness. I thought that suppressing my anger was forgiveness. I thought that not taking that kind of treatment anymore was forgiveness. *It doesn't bother me anymore, so I've obviously forgiven.* But that is not the case at all. Ignoring is not forgiving, nor is denying that it bothers you. I had to make a conscious effort to come before God and truly forgive. I had to forgive the man who molested me. I had to forgive others I felt had wronged me along the way. I had to learn to forgive for real.

I realized that this word "if" is a conditional word. I could read this scripture backwards like this: "If you do **not** forgive men their trespasses, your heavenly Father will also **not** forgive you." If you do not want to grant forgiveness, it doesn't really hurt the other person. Unforgiveness is a cancer to you. Unforgiveness will lead you down a path that you do not want to go down. It will take you further than you want to go and bring you more pain than you can imagine.

> **Then said he unto the disciples, It is impossible but that offenses will come: but woe unto him, through whom they come!**
>
> **Luke 17:1**

Again, we know that Jesus is doing the talking here because this is in red in the Bible. It is impossible for you not to be offered the temptation of being offended. People will offend you. People will try to hurt you. But that doesn't mean that you have to take it.

If someone has told you that from the moment you accept Jesus as your Lord and Savior you will no longer have any opportunity to be offended or hurt, then you have been lied to. I apologize to you on their behalf right now if anyone has said this to you. It simply isn't true.

When you were born again, it was not so people wouldn't hurt you anymore. When you were born again, it was not so you could control other people. You were born again to help you, to better you. In the new birth, you are promised eternity with God. You will be with Him forever. You are also promised a better life on this planet, but that doesn't mean that there won't be opportunities to be offended or hurt.

I think a lot of people think the faith message means that no more bad things will ever happen to them. They believe they can receive when they pray. They believe that when they speak to the mountain, it'll all go away. But the faith movement is not an escapist thing. When there is a mountain, we know how to deal with it through the Word of God and our faith. But that doesn't mean there won't be any mountains!

When dealing with forgiveness of offenses, past hurts, and people who have wronged you, you need to understand that just because you choose to forgive, doesn't mean that they won't try to do you wrong again. How you respond to their actions is your responsibility. Whether or not you continue to allow them to hold power over you based on what they have done is ultimately up to you. The ball is in your court!

For instance, in my own life, I could not stop the fact that my molester took my innocence when I was a little girl, but it was up to me whether I would allow him to control me as a 35-year-old woman. He had nothing to do with how I would respond. That's great news, if you think about it. I guarantee he wasn't thinking about me while I was agonizing through all the pain and attempting to kill myself. It was up to me to stop the insanity. I had to break the power that he had over me.

That is why you have to take a real look at forgiveness — truly forgiving. There are many consequences to unforgiveness, more than just the spiritual ones. Spiritually, Jesus said that if you won't forgive, then God won't forgive you. You don't want to ever put yourself in that place with God!

But beyond the spiritual implications, there are also relational consequences and physical consequences to unforgiveness such as increased risk for cardio-vascular problems such as strokes, heart attacks, and hypertension; poor immune function; problems with build-up of cortisol in the body; and the list goes on and on. Medical science has actually shown that having too much cortisol in the body for too long a time creates mutated cells — also known as cancer. (You might have heard of Dr. Colbert? He has traced back a lot of cancers to a root of unforgiveness. Check him out at www.drcolbert.com.) There are mental health consequences to unforgiveness including: depression, anxiety, obsessive thoughts, PTSD, and psycho-physical effects, to name a few.

Learning to Forgive

How do you forgive? Is there a forgiveness process? There is not one "right" way to forgive; forgiveness is an individual process that can be different for each person. It may look different depending on one's personality, history, and the level of hurt or trauma experienced. However, you can learn some basic steps that will help you make sense of the process and begin your journey to forgiveness.

Forgiveness is an act of faith. Underline that, circle it, whatever you need to do. If you've been hurt, you're not really going to feel — in your own nature — a desire to forgive that person who hurt you. That's most certainly not what the enemy wants you to do. But forgiveness is not about how you feel.

Offering forgiveness does not mean you condone what that person did to you. It's not letting them off the hook. It's actually letting you off the hook — the devil's hook! You have to approach forgiveness with that same bulldog-determination that we've been talking about. You have to be bulldog-determined that you're going to be healed, that you're going to have control over your soul, that you are going be obedient to the Word of God and forgive that person.

Forgiving takes faith. This is a very elementary way of looking at it, but here is a five-step process that truly works.[1] Let it guide you to a place of freedom and peace through forgiveness at a level you've never known before.

Step 1: Recall the hurt.

I just want you to recall the general hurt. Don't bring up and dwell on specific pictures that are painful or uncomfortable for you. I don't want you to feed on it. I don't want it to eat at you. I don't want the enemy to start making you uncomfortable with it. Just recall the general hurt, enough to know what you're dealing with.

---

1 Excerpts taken from R.E.A.C.H. Program from Light University/ American Association of Christian Counselors "Letting Go of Past Hurts" Spiritual Foundations Class, Everett Worthington, Jr., M.S.N.E., Ph.D.

Step 2: Emotionally replace the negative unforgiving emotion with a positive other-oriented emotion.

Let me explain how I did this in my life. I recalled my hurt — I was molested as a child. Then I took that negative event, and I said, "I can use this to help people. No, this wasn't the best scenario for my life. No, this was not the plan of God for my life. But I can choose to make this stumbling block into a stepping stone. I can choose to step up on this, be bold enough to talk about it when it's a taboo subject in church (where a lot of people don't show their issues because they want to appear perfect). I am going to put myself out there. I'm going to be vulnerable. I am going to talk about it so that I can help other people. I'm going to start looking at it from a positive place, from a higher place."

In Isaiah 55:8-9, God reveals something important.

For my thoughts are not your thoughts, neither are your ways my ways, saith the Lord. For as the heavens are higher than the earth, so are my ways higher than your ways, and my thoughts than your thoughts.

That's God talking. But He's not a big old God who is far, far away. He's not saying, "I've got thoughts you're not thinking! Na na na na na na! I've got ways above yours! You can't ever find them!" No! That's not how God is!

In the second chapter of Ephesians, Paul says that when Jesus died, He took the keys of death, hell, and the grave. When He arose into Heaven and sat down at the right hand of the Father, you were seated there with Him. You are seated above all principalities, powers, and rulers of the darkness. You have a seat! When you look to your left, you've got Jesus there. When you look to His left, there's God the Father.

You were seated high above all this earthy stuff, therefore, you can look down on your situation and rule and reign over it. Yes, you can rule and reign over what you are allowed to think. As you sit next to Jesus and next to God, and God says, "My thoughts are higher than your thoughts; My ways are higher than your ways," remember that you are seated right next to Him. You can ask Him, "Hey, what's Your thought on this matter?" And He will tell you!

My mom calls that "taking the higher thought." In every situation in your life, there is a low thought and there is a high thought. There is a low-level thought that we definitely choose to believe first. But there is a higher thought for every single situation in your life. There is a higher thought for the forgiveness you need to give to that person or persons who have hurt you. There is always a higher thought there.

Step 3: Give an altruistic gift of forgiveness.

This step is not always possible. If you are familiar with John Bevere and his *The Bait of Satan* curriculum, then you know his story. A minister hurt him, and the Holy Ghost told him to buy that person a gift. Think about that! The Holy Ghost told him to buy the person who hurt him an altruistic gift. That word "altruistic" simply means selfless. When you give an altruistic gift, it means that you're not giving to make them like you. You're not in it to make them change. You're not trying to make them feel bad. You're not in it for any other reason than you need to put yourself in a place of wanting to be a blessing.

Now for the molester and that situation in my life, I didn't have an opportunity to do this. I didn't know where he was; I still don't.

You might not have an opportunity either, but ask the Father if you are supposed to do that. In your daily journal, as you are thinking about these things and working through your healing process, write down what you would do if you did have the opportunity. Ask the Father for a higher thought concerning what you would do.

Step 4: Commit to the forgiveness that you experienced.

Allow the hurt and pain to fall away. Trust God in your journey of forgiveness. Give it your full time and attention. When the old, bad feelings of unforgiveness creep back up (and chances are they will), go through the process again. Make the choice daily to walk in forgiveness.

When you read about the apostle Peter in the gospels, you learn that he had a fiery personality. He was so very human! In his younger years with Jesus, he was always ready to jump in and do the rash thing. He led with his emotions so often. One day, he asked Jesus about this forgiveness thing. Look at Jesus' answer.

> **Then came Peter to him, and said, Lord, how oft shall my brother sin against me, and I forgive him? till seven times? Jesus saith unto him, I say not unto thee, Until seven times: but, until seventy times seven.**
>
> **Matthew 18:21-22**

Did you see that? Peter thought he was being generous by suggesting to forgive seven times, but Jesus said to forgive as many as 490 times! That's how very essential it is for you to forgive. It is truly a deep part of walking in the love of God. If you read 1 Corinthians chapter 13, especially in the *Amplified* version, you will get a really clear picture of what it looks like for you to walk in the love of God. Part of the fifth verse says:

(God's love in us) does not insist on its own rights or its own way, for it is not self-seeking; it is not touchy or fretful or resentful; it takes no account of the evil done to it [pays no attention to a suffered wrong].

You can only achieve this love walk by faith and by yielding to the Lord in your life. But the first step from where you are right now toward that place of total freedom is to forgive — 490 times a day, if you have to! Stick with it, and you will walk free and stay free of all the pain and entanglement of the past. You will walk in victory!

Step 5: Hold onto that forgiveness whenever you doubt that you have forgiven.

Of course, the devil will come at you with his thoughts, ideas, and suggestions. He will tell you that you have not really forgiven that person. He'll tell you that it's not really working. But hold onto that forgiveness whenever those doubts come. This is a process and it's done by faith. I promise you, on the other side of this forgiveness is a freedom like you have never known before! It is a freedom that I cannot express to you. You must experience it for yourself.

I went through this process about ten years ago. Then about three years ago, I was at a wedding, and lo and behold, guess who walked in the back door? Mister molester himself. At first, I was startled. I hadn't seen him since I was a kid, so it threw me for a second. But then I remembered these forgiveness steps. In that moment, I held onto that forgiveness — even though there was a split second of doubt that I had truly forgiven him. I walked up to him to shake his hand. He looked down at the floor when he saw me coming. I smiled and said, "Hey, do you remember who I am? I'm all grown up now. It's Kylie!" He knew exactly who I was. Then I said, "I hope you're doing well; I truly do," and then I walked away.

In my heart, I really do want him to be well. I want him to live a good life. I know he's been in and out of prison for years, but I want him to know God the way I know Him. When I shook his hand, I swear to you, I felt absolutely no hard feelings. There was actually quite a bit of compassion that came over me for him. The images, the imaginations, the pictures that the devil had held in front of my face for years and years absolutely had no hold on me anymore. I was free!

How did I get there? I decided to make a framework in my mind and tell my mind what I am allowed to think and what I was not allowed to think. I decided to forgive by faith. I didn't give the man a present because I didn't have the opportunity. I just saw him for a brief moment, but I did go to him and shake his hand. At that moment, I knew I was free.

He couldn't look into my eyes, and this let me know that he was very broken. I knew he was sorry for what he had done. He had not found freedom, but it was a moment of freedom for me!

Maybe you'll never see that person again who has wronged you, regardless, your freedom depends on you — not anyone else! You can't blame anybody else for holding you in this place anymore. You can't be a victim anymore. Your freedom depends on you because you have this sure word of freedom that belongs to you.

I can't begin to tell you how good it feels to be free! But I can tell you with a 100 percent guarantee that if you do the Word, you get the results of the Word. I can tell you that more people have died over the Bible, God's Word, than any other book in history. More blood has been shed over this one book. Why? Because freedom lives in this book. Everything you have need of for your victory on a daily basis lives in this process based on Scripture.

I promise you, if you'll do it, you'll see results. Though I once was a person who was diagnosed with borderline personality disorder, who was on all kinds of meds, who tried to kill herself over and over again, who was in and out of mental hospitals — I am now healed, restored, and free. I've gone back to school and received my master's degree in Christian Counseling, and I want to spend my life helping others escape the issues that plagued me for so long.

I'm sharing my story to give you hope. If you have hope, then you have something to attach your faith to. And if you have something to attach your faith to, you'll be bulldog-determined to change one step at a time. When you go to bed tonight, when you wake up tomorrow, when you wake up the next day—rejoice because you are one step closer to your freedom!

CHAPTER

6

Stirring Your Pots

Let's talk about fear. According to the Word of God, it is possible for you to live free from fear. You might be thinking, *No way! That's impossible!* Take a look at the news headlines today, and you'll see that fear rides high all around. And yet, the Bible is filled with examples of God saying to His people, "Fear not!"

Fear is the root of a lot of different things. When you've attempted something and been unsuccessful, fear is the root of your refusal to try again. When you've believed for something and haven't seen it manifest yet, fear is the root of why you no longer press on in faith. When you've been hurt, fear is the root of why you no longer trust others. Fear is the root of almost any behavioral issue. It is the core of so many issues. In the natural, when fear presses in, it's difficult to see anything but that fear. It seems like it's everywhere around you. In order to see it for what it truly is, you have to get up on a higher plain — that place of God's thoughts.

Brother Kenneth E. Hagin used to share about his mother. When Brother Hagin was young, his father left the family. His mother took him and his brother and went to live with her parents so they could help her raise them. During all of this, she became very depressed and had a nervous breakdown. One day she went to a doctor who gave her some really good advice, coupled with a prescription for medicine to help her with the depression.

Let me stop here and say that I am in no way against medications. What I am against is medicine without the Word of God. Sometimes people need a little help in their serotonin levels, a little leveling out in the hormones and chemical balances in their brains so they can have clarity in order to apply this biblical process. I was on meds myself for a while, but once I made a conscious effort to get on the right track, eventually with the help of my doctor, I was weaned off the medication.

No two people are exactly the same, so the road back to wholeness will vary. When I train ministers, I teach them not to just go tell somebody to stop taking their heart medicine, stop taking their asthma medicine, or whatever medication they may be on. The Bible says, "According to your faith be it unto you" (Matthew 9:29). In other words, you cannot determine where somebody else's faith is. You can only determine where your faith is.

Take an honest look in the mirror and assess where you are and how you're really doing. If you are on meds — anti-depressants or whatever it may be — don't just throw them all in the trash. If you stop some of that stuff cold turkey, you will find yourself in a worse spot than when you first started. That's the truth! Continue to take them as you work through this process. As you take your meds, mix the Word of God with them. God's Word will change you and sustain you. As you grow in faith and the knowledge of God's Word, you can slowly wean off the medications with your doctor's help. There is no condemnation in taking meds and exercising your faith as you go.

Back to my story about Brother Hagin's mom. She went on the medication and along with the meds, this Christian doctor gave her some other things to do. He told her, "Whenever you feel a spell coming on, just say, 'I refuse to be depressed. No, I'm not going to have an attack. I stand my ground in the name of Jesus.'" That's what it means to mix meds and faith. You could replace the word "depressed" in that confession with absolutely anything that you're facing. Remember the story about whisking the cream? When you start feeling something stirring up on the inside, you can say, "I refuse to be afraid. I am not going to be afraid. I stand my ground in the name of the Lord Jesus."

One day my Mimi told me, "You know, Kylie, you can play chess with God." And I said to her, "Well, Grandma, I would lose because He's smarter than me." But this chess game is not about losing to God, but about winning with God. And she showed me a passage of scripture, Philippians 4:6-9, which contains this chess game.

> **Be careful for nothing; but in every thing by prayer and supplication with thanksgiving let your requests be made known unto God.**
>
> **Philippians 4:6**

Now, the first move in this chess game is our move. We must take this first step which is found in this verse. The first step is to say, "I refuse to fear." It is not okay to be afraid or scared or anxious about anything. And the Lord is going to help you do that, but you have to make the first move. Every time a thought of anxiety, of fear, or of trepidation comes to your mind, you have to open your mouth and say with boldness, "Lord I praise You, and I thank You. I refuse to fear!" That's the first move.

> **And the peace of God, which passeth all understanding, shall keep your hearts and minds through Christ Jesus.**
>
> **Philippians 4:7**

Then the second move is God's move. Once you've made your move and declared that you refuse to fear, God says "Thank you for your move. Now it's my move." And He moves in! The peace of God, His *shalom* peace, the nothing missing, nothing broken peace of God moves in. And what does it do? It stands guard over your mind!

The pressure is off. The pressure is not on us because He stands guard! When the pressure tries to come, He says, "No, no! I'm surrounding her in perfect peace. She has nothing missing, nothing broken. Her mind is stayed on me. She chose to make a boundary on what thoughts she lets into her mind, on what she allows herself to think and feel. And because she did, I'm standing guard, and I am bringing double blessing on her life, because she refuses to fear."

Then it becomes our move again.

Finally, brethren, whatsoever things are true, whatsoever things are honest, whatsoever things are just, whatsoever things are pure, whatsoever things are lovely, whatsoever things are of good report; if there be any virtue, and if there be any praise, think on these things.

Philippians 4:8

Our next move is to realize that this verse is the boundary, the framework for our mind. When a home builder builds a house. He starts by laying the foundation. But once the foundation is laid, he has to build the framework for what the house will look like. Will it be one story or two? How many room will he put in place? This is how this verse works. Once we have our foundation, which is to be anxious for nothing and then God has brought us His perfect peace, we then have to build the framework for what we will allow our selves to think and feel.

You have to recognize that the devil doesn't want to just hurt you a little. He wants to ruin your life. He wants to destroy you. So God give is the answer to what our framework should be. Allow your mind to only think on those things that are pure, lovely, of good report or virtue or praise.

Those things, which ye have both learned, and received, and heard, and seen in me, do: and the God of peace shall be with you.

Philippians 4:9

The last move is Gods. Not only does He stand guard over our hearts, but He stays with us. You never have to go through life lacking peace. Peace is not the absence of trouble, mind you. Peace is you walking through the valley of the shadow of death and not fearing because *He is with you*! His last move is to remain.

There is a theme park in my hometown that's known for demonstrating how life used to be many years ago. When you enter the park, you feel like you've stepped back in time about a hundred years or more. Every worker there is called a citizen of Silver Dollar City, they are all dressed in costumes of that era and they do a lot of really neat things.

One thing they do in the fall is really special. They have a mule hooked up to a press filled with sugar cane. The mule walks round and round turning the mill and the process forces out the sap from the cane. Then they take the sap over to a big old cast iron skillet and boil it for eight hours to make sorghum. Do you know what sorghum is? It's a syrupy substance that is very sweet. Sorghum is good on pancakes or biscuits and you can even bake with it.

While they're boiling this sap down for eight hours, this green, nasty looking slime appears on the surface of the boiling liquid. The workers keep skimming off that nasty substance; every few minutes, they'll skim off some more. What are they doing? They are taking out the impurities. The more the sap boils, the more impurities rise to the top. By the end of that eight-hour process, there is no more of that green stuff. What is left is a clear, syrupy liquid with a nice sweet flavor to it.

Many times, when you're going through the processes of restoring your soul, stuff comes up, and it's kind of green and slimy! But as you go with the Word of God and continue through the process, you are skimming off the impurities. You skim that off so you can come to a really pure and innocent place where you tap into the things of God.

Now, if they just kept stirring that sap without skimming off the impurities, would they be successful in producing the clear, sweet product they're looking for? No. The gunk has to come out. In your own personal walk with God, you have to know what to do and when to do it to achieve the results you seek.

The Spirit of God, through the different writers of the Bible, talks a lot about stirring and having the ability to stir up things on the inside of you. In Psalm 80:2, David calls on God to "stir up thy strength, and come and save us." We know that time and time again, God did stir up His strength and came to David's aid. You are made in the image and the likeness of God, so if God can stir up strength, then you can stir up strength too!

In Isaiah 42:13, you see a picture of God stirring up jealousy "like a man of war." Jealousy, for God, is different from what we usually think of when we think of being jealous. When God is said to be jealous, it means that He wants a relationship with you, He doesn't want you putting any other gods in His place in your life, and He will stop at nothing to bring you to Him. The devil, on the other hand, stirs up a negative kind of jealousy. His kind of jealousy is covetous and divisive; you have to be aware of the dangers of the devil's jealousy. When he first comes to you, he will just plant a random thought, but if you start to dwell on that thought and stir it up instead of recognizing the enemy, judging the thought, and holding fast the framework of your mind, before long you'll have bubbles of destructive jealousy rising to the surface.

What about anger? That's something else that can be stirred up. Proverbs 15:1 says, "A soft answer turneth away wrath: but grievous words stir up anger." How you respond with the words of your mouth in any situation matters very much. You could say that the words of your mouth are the spoon or the whisk. Your words are what stir; your words are your spoon. Your words can be used to harm you and others, or you can use your words to shut up the lies of the devil. You must use your words by saying, "In the name of Jesus, I plead the blood of Jesus over my mind. I only think thoughts of life. I do not think thoughts of death. I am choosing which pot I am going to stir." You choose what you stir up!

The constant question for you is, *Which pot are you going to stir?* Are you going to stir up the pot that makes you angry by calling up Sister So-and-So to tell her how hacked off you are? Or are you going to stir up with the words of your mouth the pot that brings peace to reign in your soul? You choose to stir the peace pot by saying, "In the name of Jesus, I plead the blood of Jesus over my mind. I do not think thoughts of death. I only think thoughts of life. I refuse to be angry. I do not live in anger." The words of your mouth is the spoon that dictate which pot you are stirring, what thoughts you are going to think and when you are going to think them.

Beloved, I am now writing you this second letter. In [both of] them I have stirred up your unsullied (sincere) mind by way of remembrance.

2 Peter 3:1, AMP

Another spoon you stir with is your memory. Your memory, if not controlled, will stir up emotions, fear, anxiety, and other things that will take you down the road you do not want to travel. As your memories brings things to your mind, if you don't keep them in the proper framework, they will stir up death on the inside of you.

In this verse, Peter said he stirred up pure minds by way of remembrance. He used memory in a positive way. He stirred up peace and pure minds by reminding them what Jesus had done for them. When you find yourself stirring a pot that is starting to get you a little agitated, start remembering what Jesus has done for you. Start thinking about the blood of Jesus shed for you. Start thinking about Him going to the cross. Start thinking about all that He took on the cross for you. Stir those memories.

Do you recall what I said at the very beginning of this book? Jesus died for your mind because a renewed mind is the devil's worst nightmare. Start thinking about that. Stir up your pure mind by way of remembrance.

I am calling up memories of your sincere and unqualified faith [the leaning of your entire personality on God in Christ in absolute trust and confidence in His power, wisdom and goodness), [a faith] that first lived permanently in [the heart of] your grandmother Lois and your mother Eunice and now, I am [fully] persuaded, [dwells] in you also. That is why I would remind you to stir up (rekindle the embers of, fan the flame of, and keep burning) the [gracious] gift of

God, [the inner fire] that is in you by means of the laying on of my hands [with those of the elders at your ordination]. For God did not give us a spirit of timidity (of cowardice, of craven and cringing and fawning fear) but [He has given us a spirit] of power and of love and of a calm and well-balanced mind and discipline and self-control.

2 Timothy 1:5-7, AMP

Your Defining Moment

What is the opposite of fear? Faith. Faith and fear are polar opposites. They cannot exist in the same atmosphere. What did Paul tell Timothy to do? Before telling him that God hadn't given him a spirit of fear, he told Timothy to stir up what was on the inside of him that was given to his grandmother and mother back in the day. He told Timothy to be in remembrance, to think about what they had. You are no different. You too must stir up on the inside of you, the remembrance that God has not given you a spirit of fear.

Paul took Timothy back to a specific time when hands were laid on him at his ordination into the ministry. Paul wanted him to remember back to that point. It had been a defining moment in Timothy's life. I pray that as you go on through this process, as you're walking your own path and running your own race that God has for you, that you are able to look back to this very moment right here as you read this and know it was a defining moment in your life. As you do that, I pray you will say, "Fear may be trying to come, but I remember." Come on! Say, "I remember what Pastor Kylie said in that book!" I pray you stir that up. I pray that you go back to this place and be in remembrance.

Look at verse 7 again in the *Amplified* version. You could read this verse in reverse, which sometimes brings even more clarity to what's being said. Read in reverse, it would sound something like this: "Because He gave me a well-balanced mind, the ability to walk in discipline and self-control, I do not have a spirit of fear."

You can open your mouth and use the spoon of your words to say, "Because I have a well-balanced mind and discipline and self-control, I refuse to have a spirit of fear." That is so good! What are you doing when you do that? You are telling your mind what it is allowed to think and not think. You are positioning the two-by-fours in the framework of your mind. God said He gave you a well-balanced mind so if anybody or anything tries to tell you any different, you know that it is a lie of the enemy. You were given a package from Jesus himself, which included a well-balanced mind! Say this one more time: "Because I have a well-balanced mind, discipline, and self-control, I do not have a spirit of fear." Rejoice in that today and every day! Let it become real to you!

Keep your bulldog-determination stirred up. When you wake up in the morning, you need to say, "I'm going to be free today! I am walking in freedom!" This is not a one-time deal. It's an every day, sometimes moment-by-moment deal. It's like taking medicine; you have to faithfully take the dosage that's been prescribed. It's doing what you need to do but the thing about it is, it will set you free forever! Think about that. Say this out loud and say it often, "Self, stir up!" There's something so powerful about that.

We serve a really, really, really faithful God! Look at John 14:1 in the *Amplified*.

Do not let your hearts be troubled (distressed, agitated). You believe in and adhere to and trust in and rely on God; believe in and adhere to and trust in and rely also on Me.

The *King James* says it like this:

Let not your heart be troubled: ye believe in God, believe also in me.

The word "let" is the word for *roil*, like if you're boiling water and it starts to bubble a lot. What does that remind you of? Whipping the cream, right? The word "heart" is actually mistranslated. The Greek word actually refers to your thoughts and your feelings. It is not your spirit, but it is your thoughts and feelings — your soul. So don't let those thoughts and feelings be troubled. Don't let your soul be troubled.

The word picture that the Greek gives here is don't muddle up, don't muddy up your thoughts and feelings with trouble because it's hard to walk through the thick mud. That's really interesting, isn't it? I know you have had times when your thoughts and feelings seemed exactly like thick mud that was hard to get through.

Now let's go on into John 14:27. In this verse, Jesus is saying something very important.

Peace I leave with you, my peace I give unto you: not as the world giveth, give I unto you. Let not your heart be troubled, neither let it be afraid.

What does that say? Don't let your heart be troubled, neither let it be what? Afraid! There's that fear again! If you're afraid, it's because you allow yourself to be afraid. You must create a framework for your mind. You must tell your mind to think or not to think.

In this verse the phrase "let not your heart be troubled" in the Greek means to stir up. It's telling you not to stir up fear and trouble. Don't allow yourself to do it. So many times when you've been hurt, you've looked at your life and situation through the glasses of your hurt and pain and you've allowed yourself to be afraid. You've allowed yourself to be troubled just because you don't want to be hurt again.

But Jesus says, "Don't allow it. Let not ..." Who has that power? You do! It's in your hands. Whenever you watch the news and hear stories of financial collapse, crime, or terrorist attacks, you can sit there and allow your heart to be troubled. You can sit there and allow your thoughts to run wild and your words to speak out bad things. You can get your memories going and stir up fear and anxiety on the inside of you. Or, you can stir up your faith and your trust in God and all His promises to you in His Word. If you trust God, you will experience peace. Whose hands is that decision in? It's in your hands; it's your choice.

If you want to walk in peace, you say, "I refuse to be afraid. I refuse to walk in fear. I walk in peace." What are you doing when you stand up and say that? You are using the spoon of your words to stir up the correct pot, to stir up the pot of peace, the pot of love, the pot of a sound mind.

God loves you too much to let anything happen to you. Make much of the blood of Jesus. Go find scriptures about the blood and protection. If you need some help getting started, the books *The Blood and the Glory* and *The Authority of the Believer & How to Use It* by Billye Brim are amazing resources. Search out scriptures that talk about peace, love, trust, and restoration. God's Word is full of these things!

I could spend a lot more time teaching you about fear, this is just the short version! But just remember, you are not meant to be a victim of fear, no matter what the fear. There is a list of hundreds and hundreds of phobias that people walk in on a daily basis. You are not meant to live there. John gave you the answer for fear in one of his letters.

> **There is no fear in love; but perfect love casteth out fear: because fear hath torment. He that feareth is not made perfect in love.**
>
> **1 John 4:18**

I want you to learn this verse and repeat it out loud every time you are faced with a fearful thought or situation. In the *Amplified* it says, "He who is afraid has not reached the full maturity of love [is not yet grown into love's complete perfection]."

When John speaks of love here, he's not talking about you loving others, although that helps. What he's talking about is receiving the love that God has for you. There is no fear in love. If you are in a position where you feel true love, you are not going to fear in that situation. I personally have no doubt that my husband, Jimmy Gatewood, will be faithful to me. Why? Because I know that he loves me! I have no doubt that he loves me, so I don't have any fear. Whenever love is in question, fear is always in operation.

Remember, human love will fail. Human love always has certain limitations, but God's love is limitless. His love never fails. As you continue to experience the love of God more and more, fear will become less and less of an issue for you.

Say this out loud right now, and mean it: "I receive the love of God. I bind the thoughts of the enemy that say I don't deserve that love. I do deserve that love. Jesus made it possible for me to deserve the love of God. I receive the love of God which casts out all fear, in Jesus' name."

Before you leave this space, take a few moments to close your eyes and allow God's love to permeate every cell of your being. He wants you to experience Him in ways you've never experienced Him before. He loves you so much.

CHAPTER

7

Relabeling Yourself

If I want to get to know who you are, you might give me all kinds of information about yourself. You might say you're tall or short, male or female, large or small. You might throw in your skin color or tell me who your parents are. You might try to tell me who you are by telling me what you do, whether you're a single mom or a professional of some kind. You might have picked up a label or two along the way from any number of places; labels such as *slow, stupid, inferior, poor, worthless,* nobody are terribly painful and do much damage. Labels can deeply affect how you think about yourself, how you treat yourself, and what you choose to pursue in your life.

Labels are everywhere. Look around in your life, and identify the labels that you find.

Not all labels that people — and you yourself — attach to you are pleasant or even true. I want to help strip off those old hurtful, lying labels and help you relabel yourself. *How can I do that?* I'm glad you asked! You're going to do it by learning what God's Word says about you.

If everyone else in your life can put a label on you, surely God can. What do you think God's label for you might look like? God doesn't label you the same way the world does. He has labeled you through His Word with verses that are known as the "In Him" realities. You'll find these verses by going through the New Testament scriptures, looking for scriptures that say "in Christ," *in Him,* or *in Whom.*

That ye put off concerning the former conversation the old man, which is corrupt according to the deceitful lusts; and be renewed in the spirit of your mind; and that ye put on the new man, which after God is created in righteousness and true holiness. Wherefore putting away lying, speak every man truth with his neighbour: for we are members one of another. Be ye angry, and sin not: let not the sun go down upon your wrath.

Ephesians 4:22-26

What does this passage mean? You can't talk the way you used to talk. You can't have the conversations you used to have. In the Greek, the word "conversation" is also "behaviors." This is telling you to put off the old ways and conversations — the old lifestyle — because it is corrupted, and be renewed in your mind. You are told to put off the old and put on the new man, which is like God in righteousness and holiness.

It's just like the way you take off your clothes at night and put on your pajamas. This act requires effort, but you can do it. You put off the old man, and you put on the new man. Did you notice some of the things you have to put away? You have to put away lying and begin to speak truth with people in your life. You are instructed to be angry and not sin. How do you do that? You can get mad, but you don't sin about it. Keep your mouth closed if you have to. Don't let the sun go down on your anger. If you're mad at your husband or wife, make sure you clear it up before you go to bed.

These words totally apply to your life today. Don't give place to the devil. Don't give him any ground. If you've stolen, don't steal anymore. Instead, work with your hands what is good so you will have money to take care of yourself and to give to others. Watch what comes out of your mouth. Put a guard on your mouth, and speak what is good and edifying to others. Let your words minister grace to those who hear them. Again, think about the words of your mouth as being a spoon to stir up either the pot of all this junk or the pot of love and grace. Let no corrupt communication proceed out of your mouth. This will help make happy paths for your feet so you can overcome the battle of your soul.

In verse 25, the *Amplified* version tells us, "Therefore, rejecting all falsity and being done now with it, let everyone express the truth with his neighbor." You have to come to the point in your bulldog determination that you decide you are finished with the old way now. It's over. That will be one of your defining moments. Write it across the top of your calendar, "Today, I'm done with all this stuff. Today, I'm done with lying. Today, I'm done with corrupt communication. Today, I'm done with that weight or that sin that so easily besets me."

Ephesians 4:27 in the *Amplified* version says, "Leave no [such] room or foothold for the devil [give no opportunity to him]." Why is that important? Because by doing so, you are closing off any opportunities for the devil to operate in your life. Praise the Lord! That is great news!

Relabel yourself. You might be known as a liar. Maybe you were known as a cheater or as someone not to be trusted. You might have dealt with insecurity issues. All through life, you may have been marked with these different labels. But you have the option to relabel yourself! Strip away the old labels, and put on new ones based on how God sees you, on what He says about you. You can learn what these new labels should be by searching for them in the Word of God.

> **Being justified freely by his grace through the redemption that is in Christ Jesus.**
>
> **Romans 3:24**

What do you do with scriptures like this? You make them personal to you. In this case, you could say, "I am justified and made upright in Christ." Personalizing scriptures like this combats all those dumb thoughts like, *I'm a nobody, I'm worthless.* No! No! In Christ, you are justified and made upright!

> **Even so consider yourselves also dead to sin and your relation to it broken, but alive to God [living in unbroken fellowship with Him] in Christ Jesus.**
>
> **Romans 6:11, AMP**

Based on this scripture, you can say this: "I am dead unto sin and alive unto Christ." Come on! When you're even tempted to sin, that is a great confession.

One of my favorite scriptures is Romans 8:1, because I had to live on that one.

> **There is therefore now no condemnation to them which are in Christ Jesus, who walk not after the flesh, but after the Spirit.**

Take that scripture right now and make it your own by saying it out loud where you can hear it. Say, "I take it now. There is no condemnation on me. I live and walk from my spirit and not from my flesh." What are you doing when you say this? You are using that spoon of your words to stir up the pot of who you really are! Say, "I am not condemned. I do not receive condemnation. I walk and live after the spirit and not after the flesh."

Romans 8:2 follows right along with that verse:

For the law of the Spirit of life in Christ Jesus hath made me free from the law of sin and death.

Can you guess what you need to do with this verse? The same as you did with the others. You say it out loud and make it your own. Say, "The law of the Spirit of life in Christ has made me free from the law of sin and death." Say it like you mean it! Don't just say it once and forget it. These confessions must become a regular part of your daily life. Victory comes in the moment-to-moment, not in the once-in-awhile of what you do and say.

So we, being many, are one body in Christ, and every one members one of another.

Romans 12:5

We, numerous as we are, are one body in Christ, and individually we are parts one to another. We are mutually dependent on one another. Why do you need to be whole in your soul? Because there are other peoples' lives depending on you being whole in your soul. No one is an island.

Unto the church of God which is at Corinth, to them that are sanctified in Christ Jesus, called to be saints, with all

that in every place call upon the name of Jesus Christ our Lord, both their's and our's.

1 Corinthians 1:2

With this verse, you can say, "I am holy in Christ Jesus." You may not feel holy, but even if you don't feel or look holy, you say, "I am holy in Christ Jesus. I am relabeling myself." It is so important for you to get this. It is life changing. It is agreeing with God about yourself, and it brings freedom.

I thank my God always on your behalf, for the grace of God which is given you by Jesus Christ.

1 Corinthians 1:4

What can you say based on this verse? "I walk in grace. I walk in favor. I walk in blessing in Christ Jesus. I am relabeling myself. I am a blessed person. I am a favored person in Jesus' name!" In this simple way, you are changing your labels. You are changing what you believe about yourself to match what God says about you.

But of him are ye in Christ Jesus, who of God is made unto us wisdom, and righteousness, and sanctification, and redemption.

1 Corinthians 1:30

Say, "I'm redeemed from sin. I'm made right in Christ." With verses like this, you can successfully combat all the thoughts, ideas, and suggestions that the devil tries to bring your way.

For as in Adam all die, even so in Christ shall all be made alive.

1 Corinthians 15:22

Based on the promise of this verse you can say, "I am alive in Christ — not just surviving, but living in Him!"

Now thanks be unto God, which always causeth us to triumph in Christ, and maketh manifest the savour of his knowledge by us in every place.

2 Corinthians 2:14

If the devil tries to lie to you saying, "You're always a loser. You lose everything — every relationship and good thing that comes your way," you have a powerful answer for him. Tell the devil with your voice, "Thanks be to God, Who in Christ always leads me in triumph!" That's what the *Amplified* version says. You can always say what The *Message Bible* says, too: "God leads me from place to place in one perpetual victory parade!" You'll feel the power of those words just by saying them!

Therefore if any person is [ingrafted] into Christ (the Messiah) he is a new creation (a new creature altogether); the old [previous moral and spiritual condition] has passed away. Behold, the fresh and new has come!"

2 Corinthians 5:17, AMP

Oh, that one is fun to say! "The old man has passed away. The old way of thinking has passed away. Behold, I have become new!" Go to this scripture and speak it and think about it rather than dwelling on the lies that the devil throws up in your face about where you've been and what you've done. You tell him, "I'm a whole new being in Christ Jesus. All that old junk has passed away! God's not looking at it, and I'm not either! All my old has been made new!"

That becomes shouting ground there!

It was God [personally present] in Christ, reconciling and restoring the world to favor with Himself, not counting up and holding against [men] their trespasses [but cancelling them], and committing to us the message of reconciliation (of the restoration to favor).

2 Corinthians 5:19, AMP

Ephesians 3:6	*1 Thessalonians 4:16*	*2 Timothy 2:1*
Philippians 3:14	*1 Thessalonians 5:18*	*2 Timothy 2:10*
Philippians 4:7	*1 Timothy 1:1*	*2 Timothy 3:15*
Philippians 4:13	*1 Timothy 1:14*	*Philemon 1:6*
Philippians 4: 19	*2 Timothy 1:9*	*1 Peter 5:10*
Colossians 4:19	*2 Timothy 1:13*	

I've listed for you above most of the "in Christ" scriptures. There are lots more in Scripture that are "in Him" and "in Whom." I really encourage you to look up all of those on your own, and for your convenience, they are located at the end of this chapter. Learning these truths from God's Word — the truths about you — gives you an excellent foundation for bringing your soul under control.

You have to speak the truth about who you are in Christ daily. I like to start out doing this first thing in the morning, which might mean you have to get up a few minutes earlier, but it is well worth the little inconvenience. Continue speaking this truth throughout the entire day. Setting God as first place in your life always helps you win the battle.

(For the weapons of our warfare are not carnal, but mighty through God to the pulling down of strong holds;) Casting down imaginations, and every high thing that exalteth itself against the knowledge of God, and bringing into captivity every thought to the obedience of Christ.

2 Corinthians 10:4-5

God tells you to take on the mindset of a battle-seasoned soldier fighting the enemy. The thoughts that trouble you will not be conquered by ignoring them any more than a soldier can conquer his enemy by ignoring him. The soldier faces his enemy and fights him. So be ready with your battle gear in place. Be ready with your breastplate of righteousness, your helmet of salvation, and your shield of faith; and be ready to fight (Ephesians 6). Your daily walk is a fight, but I promise you, it gets easier if you do the Word. Say, "If I do the Word, I will live free!" It's true for you!

In Christ Scriptures

Ephesians 3:6
That the Gentiles should be fellowheirs, and of the same body, and partakers of his promise in Christ by the gospel:

Philippians 3:14
I press toward the mark for the prize of the high calling of God in Christ Jesus.

Philippians 4:7
And the peace of God, which passeth all understanding, shall keep your hearts and minds through Christ Jesus.

Philippians 4:13
I can do all things through Christ which strengtheneth me.

Philippians 4:19
But my God shall supply all your need according to his riches in glory by Christ Jesus.

Colossians 1:2b
...that we may present every man perfect in Christ Jesus.

1 Thessalonians 4:16
For the Lord himself shall descend from heaven with a shout, with the voice of the archangel, and with the trump of God: and the dead in Christ shall rise first:

1 Thessalonians 5:18
In every thing give thanks: for this is the will of God in Christ Jesus concerning you.

1 Timothy 1:14
And the grace of our Lord was exceeding abundant with faith and love which is in Christ Jesus. .

2 Timothy 1:9
Who hath saved us, and called us with an holy calling, not according to our works, but according to his own purpose and grace, which was given us in Christ Jesus before the world began,

2 Timothy 1:13
Hold fast the form of sound words, which thou hast heard of me, in faith and love which is in Christ Jesus.

2 Timothy 2:1
Thou therefore, my son, be strong in the grace that is in Christ Jesus.

2 Timothy 2:10
Therefore I endure all things for the elect's sakes, that they may also obtain the salvation which is in Christ Jesus with eternal glory.

2 Timothy 3:15
And that from a child thou hast known the holy scriptures, which are able to make thee wise unto salvation through faith which is in Christ Jesus.

Philemon 1:6
That the communication of thy faith may become effectual by the acknowledging of every good thing which is in you in Christ Jesus.

1 Peter 5:10
But the God of all grace, who hath called us unto his eternal glory by Christ Jesus, after that ye have suffered a while, make you perfect, stablish, strengthen, settle you.

CHAPTER

8

Staying Free: The Daily Walk

Learning to let your spirit take the higher place over your mind, will, and emotions is truly a journey, not a destination. You can read this book cover to cover without experiencing any change whatsoever in your life. If you are counting on merely having the information and being free, I have to tell you that it doesn't work that way. Remember, it's not what you know; it's what you do that counts. That is still as true as ever!

It works if you do the steps. It won't be easy, and it will take some effort on your part, but if you stay with the process, you will be free!

One of the greatest things you can do for yourself as you work through this process is to stay hooked up in your walk with Jesus. A great way to receive encouragement is to follow me on my website at www.kyliegatewood.com.

There you will find a link that I have posted for you. The link will take you to a little mini-book called *No Fear Here* by Pastor

George Pearsons. It's a free download. The book is 33 little bitty pages. It took me about ten minutes to read it. It is chocked full of scriptures dealing with fear and being set free from fear. Pastor Pearsons wrote the book right after 9/11 terrorist attacks and the anthrax scare. He offers three simple steps for dealing with fear:

1) Accept Jesus as your Lord and Savior

2) Tell fear to get out of your life right now

3) Come to church and learn more

Can it really be that simple? Yes! The enemy tries to complicate everything, but the things of God are very simple and straightforward. It is true that when you isolate yourself, it is a lot easier to lose control. But when you keep yourself around like-minded believers, you will find much strength, and that helps you very much.

I want to show you how to not give up, lose heart, or faint in your walk to gain control of your soul. Let's take a look again at one of the letters the apostle Paul wrote. I want you to see from the Word of God that you are not alone!

Therefore then, since we are surrounded by so great a cloud of witnesses [who have borne testimony to the Truth], let us strip off and throw aside every encumbrance (unnecessary weight) and that sin which so readily (deftly and cleverly) clings to and entangles us, and let us run with patient endurance and steady and active persistence the appointed course of the race that is set before us.

Hebrews 12:1, AMP

Who are these witnesses spoken of in this verse? They are those who have gone on before who are interested in your life, that's who. And there are a lot of them!

There is a minister named Dr. Gary Wood. He has written a book called *A Place Called Heaven* about his experience in Heaven. He died in a car accident when he was a teenager and was dead for over 45 minutes. It is all documented. The medical team stopped working on him. He was cold. That was it. They gave up on him. He was gone. He tells about it with more detail in his book. (You can purchase his book at www.BillyeBrim.org.)

Dr. Wood saw many things when he visited Heaven. At one point, he was taken to a place that was like an arena. Out in the middle of the arena where a playing field would normally be, there was instead something like a portal that looked down onto the earth. People would go to the arena, and they would hang over the side. From there, they could see different loved ones and various people whom God had put on their hearts, and they were cheering them on from above. He heard them saying things like: "You can do it! You can do it, dude! Come on! Run! Run! Run! You can do it! You can do it!"

These people in Heaven who were viewing events on earth didn't know little everyday things like what you had for lunch, but they were able to see big spiritual advancements or retreats. They knew if you weren't doing what you needed to do, and they knew when you were advancing too. He said they knew of big things like weddings and big life events, and they would lean over the banisters in that arena and yell, "You can do it! Kylie, come on! Run! Run, Kylie, run!" They were cheering; this huge cloud of witnesses were all cheering for someone on the earth!

Guess what. This might sound pretty wild to you, but we just read it in the Word of God! Every one of us has somebody on the other side cheering for us. You have people there cheering for you. Whether or not you are family to them, God has placed a cloud of witnesses, a cheering section for you, saying, "You can overcome this soul stuff! You can do it! You can make it! You can be victorious! Come on! Run, baby, run! Open your mouth! Do what you need to do! Put it all together! You can do it! You can do it! You can do it!"

Aren't you glad you're not here by yourself? Aren't you glad that for every moment of every day in heaven, someone is cheering for you? Somebody is cheering just for you! The struggle might have been real, but someone is cheering for you saying, "You can do this! You can overcome by the blood of the Lamb, by the word of your testimony! You love your life not to the death! You can do it! You don't have to live like that anymore!"

Since we have this cheering section in Heaven, God says we should strip off and throw aside every encumbrance and sin. That's interesting. Notice that not every encumbrance is a sin, but it can still be a weight to us. What we're dealing with can be a sin that's been tripping us up, or it can just be a weight to us. We won't fully gain control of our souls if we don't take an honest look at our lives. Start looking at everything and determine if it is a weight and if it is a sin that has tried to keep you from running the way you need to run in your life.

I had to place upon the altar of God, the sexual immorality of my life. It was a sin that was causing me to mess up. It was keeping me from running the race that I needed to run. I had to choose to take off that sin, just like this verse says.

Today, with your cheering section rooting for you, take an

honest look at yourself and ask, "What weight is holding me back?" Another word for encumbrance is *distraction,* so you could ask what distraction is holding you back. Who is a distraction to you? What person in your life is not lifting you up, but is instead jacking you up?

My husband is so smart! He says you should never be the smartest person in the room. You should always surround yourself with people who can pull you up. If you look at a room filled with people you're having to lift up because they're not living right or they're not doing right, I would say you need to sever some relationships because you need to be around people who are lifting you up. There were friendships I had to sever. It was painful, but I knew that the ones going with me to the bar right after I got off work were not the ones who were going to carry me to victory. My relationships with them weren't necessarily a sin, but they were a distraction, a weight to me.

You have to take an honest account of your life. Some people around you are dealing with soul issues themselves, and if you're dealing with soul issues, you can't be around those people. You need somebody who has a better handle on how to control these areas of his soul. This is not a cute or popular part of this message, but it is extremely needful. Amen? Unhealthy relationships are unnecessary weights that will keep you from gaining the freedom you desire.

In Hebrews 12:1 above, circle the words "throw aside." In the Greek, those words carry the idea of throwing aside with the intensity of a bullet coming out of a gun. That's pretty fast! It's not a matter of, "Well, let me think about it for a while. Let me think about Susie. You know, she's been a friend for 20 years. I can't just get rid of her, you know." The truth is, Susie's not doing anything for you. There has to come a point where you want to be free so badly, that you say, "No hard feelings, Susie. If you get right, praise the Lord. I'm praying for you, but I have to run my race. I have to do what God has called me to do. And with the intensity and power of a bullet coming out of a gun, I'm laying down this extra weight and I'm running."

What does it mean to run with patient endurance? It means you might not see 100 percent victory and total freedom by tonight, but you're going to keep running. Endurance is to keep on trucking, to be steady and keep on trucking. Don't stop.

My husband ran marathons before we got married, then he had a foot injury, so he stopped. After I had our baby, I wanted to lose weight, so he said, "Alright. I signed us up for this 5K." I was thinking, *Uh, what?* Now you must know that in school, I was the kid in class who thought of every possible way to not run during Phys-Ed. Now here was my husband saying, "Okay, I've signed us up for a 5K."

I said, "Um, okay baby, that's great." And he said, "We're going to go shopping, and we're going to practice, and we're going to work your way up. But first, we're definitely going shopping." Well, you know I'm not ever going to complain about going shopping! But then I asked him why we were going shopping. He answered, "Because I don't want you to look like a novice." He went on to explain to me that there's a very distinct difference between the person who comes to win the race and the one who comes to just experience the race.

The first thing he said we had to change was my socks. That seemed kind of silly to me. "Yes, we have to change your socks because if you're really going to run, you don't want blisters.

You can't have socks with a lot of cotton in them. Cotton causes blisters."(See, I'm teaching you something here today!) I did not know that about cotton socks.

We got synthetic socks, and we got a certain kind of shoes so my knees wouldn't hurt. We also bought a certain kind of pants and shirt. And then we practiced. *A lot.* I showed up at the race that day thinking I probably wasn't going to run the whole 5K, but I was going to run the majority of it, and I knew I was going to be all right.

When I got there, I looked around, and it was just exactly the way Jimmy said it would be. I saw two very distinctly different groups of people. The one group was dressed in the best running gear they could find. They had on their special watches, and they were getting ready to set them. They were jogging before the race even started — you know those people are crazy! They were totally into it and prepared for it.

And then there was the second group. They were wearing their race t-shirt, a pair of basketball shorts, and some basketball trainers — you know what I'm talking about. Those people were there for the fun of it, but they were not there to win.

The biggest difference between these two groups was this: the runners in both groups would likely hurt along the way, but those in the first group could run through the pain. They could continue running even if they started to feel a little uncomfortable. They could run through it, and eventually the pain could knock off. They could keep going.

Those in the second group, however, when they experienced some kind of little pain would stop running. The pain stopped them. It would hinder their time, their race, and where they would finish. Those in the first group learned endurance while those in the second group were just there for the experience.

Which runner are you in this race called life? Are you here to win it? Over and over again, the Apostle Paul talks about being in a race. You have to ask yourself which category fits you. Are you running the appointed course with patient endurance, with steady and active persistence? Underline "appointed course" in Hebrews 12:1. It's not talking about somebody else's course; it's talking about your course. What are *you* called to do? You can usually look at your passions and the things that you're good at to find an answer to that question. The Lord will somehow have those wrapped up in what you're called to do.

It's your race. There's a grace for your lane. There's a grace for your race. There's a grace for your place. If you're running somebody else's race or crossing over into another lane, you'll feel like something is just off. Dr. Hagin used to say, "It's like washing your feet with your socks on — something's just a little bit off." Take a look at what race you are running. What are you doing? What lane are you in, and how are you running?

> **Looking away [from all that will distract] to Jesus, Who is the Leader and the Source of our faith [giving the first incentive for our belief] and is also its Finisher, [bringing it to maturity and perfection]. He, for the joy [of obtaining the prize] that was set before Him, endured the cross, despising and ignoring the shame, and is now seated at the right hand of the throne of God.**
>
> **Hebrews 12:2, AMP**

Do you know what brought Jesus through the passion that He had to go through? It was the joy that was set before Him — that joy was your face and my face. We are the joy that was set before Jesus. You are the joy that was set before Jesus! Think about that. Let it settle in you for a moment. Wrap your heart around that. You gave Him so much joy that He endured all of the lashing, all of the beating, all of the piercing, all of the nailing, all of the hanging, all of the death, hell, and the grave. Your face was there so that you could be the joy set before Him. He died so you could run, so we could all run. He absolutely did that for you and me and everyone else!

What is the joy set before you to run this race and to control your soul? Ask the Father. What is the thing that will motivate you? For me, I would not have been happy if I couldn't sing and lead people into the presence of God. Even in the lowest of my low times, it is what I always wanted to do. Even when I was running from God's call on my life, the joy of that feeling has always been there. I've been ministering in church since I was three years old. I can't remember my first message, it was so long ago, but I knew that I really loved that feeling. So when I was going through the daily necessities of the daily, I would remember that feeling as the joy set before me. When I was saying my confessions up to 200 times a day, I would have that in mind.

As I gained more and more control over my soul — mind, will and emotions — I was more and more able to start loving on people the way I wanted to. Why? Because I experienced the love of God in a new way. I knew that in my deepest and lowest point, He actually never left me. That moment when I sat in the corner of the mental facility on a hard wooden chair with a blanket around me, and I said, "God," He said, "Yep." He was there for me. He never left me. He never forsook me. He never gave up on me. He looked ahead to this point in my life today, to 35-year-old Kylie who has her happy back, and that's who He saw when I was in that chair. That's how He looks at you, too!

I wanted to help people. That was the joy set before me. I also really wanted to be married, and I wanted to have a family. I didn't want to pass on generational curses to my child. There was a reason why I woke up every morning and stayed determined, and there has to be a reason why you wake up every morning and stay determined. That was all out there. Jesus had the joy set before Him to cause Him to endure. You have a joy. You have to see the joy before you to can endure while you're learning to control your soul. See that thing that motivates you.

My mother had kind of an inferiority complex at one time. People would call her and ask her to preach, and she'd say, "No, no you don't want me. You want my mother; she's famous." She didn't feel worthy enough, and the devil was trying to keep her in a very low place with her voice silent.

One night she had a vision. She saw this pasture with beautiful rolling hills, almost like pictures you've seen of Ireland. She was walking over these gentle hills when, all of a sudden, she saw a beautiful stream. There was a man crouched down by the stream, and he was working very intently on something. She came closer and closer until she could peek over the shoulder of this man. In his hands, she saw this grotesque, ugly, cancerous-looking thing.

As she watched, he would sweep down and dip his hand into the water. Then he would allow the water to run over his fingers and drop on this nasty thing. Wherever the water dropped, healing would come. Like new baby skin, it would come.

Then she looked closer at the man and took a step back. Suddenly she realized it was Jesus. She said, "What are You doing? What is that ugly nasty thing?"

Jesus looked up at her and said, "That's your soul. I am the Great

Shepherd, and I want to restore your soul."

Mom asked, "Well, what do I do to keep it from being like that?" Jesus then walked her through much of the process I have shared with you in this book.

> **He refreshes and restores my life (my self); He leads me in the paths of righteousness[uprightness and right standing with Him – not for my earning it, but] for His name's sake. Yes, though I walk through the [deep, sunless] valley of the shadow of death, I will fear or dread no evil, for You are with me; Your rod [to protect] and Your staff [to guide], they comfort me. You prepare a table before me in the presence of my enemies. You anoint my head with oil; my [brimming] cup runs over. Surely or only goodness, mercy, and unfailing love shall follow me all the days of my life, and through the length of my days the house of the Lord [and His presence] shall be my dwelling place.**

> **Psalm 23, AMP**

Look at that. Jesus leads you beside still and restful waters. I declare right now in the name of Jesus, if you are having trouble sleeping, that He leads you beside still and restful waters. You tell your soul to stop with the lies, and you will sleep!

He refreshes and restores your life. He leads you in paths of righteousness, uprightness and right standing with Him, not because you earned it, but for His name's sake. All of these things must be part of your daily soul care as you learn to walk in the freedom Jesus died to give you. It's a daily thing. Hold fast. Bring to remembrance the good He has done for you. Confess the Word. Stay connected. Soul Control is yours for the taking!

A Parent's Perspective

I have been open and bold in sharing my experience of Soul Control with you. You have had a glimpse of me at my worst! I believe at this time it is worth saying that you now know more about where I was and what I was doing and going through during that period of time than my parents or any family members did.

If you're like I was, going through your own issues and pain, you may be hiding out from your family and loved ones. You may choose to do this, and that's okay. God loves you and works with you right where you are. He certainly did with me. That's good news! But I know from my own experience and from ministering to so many others in this same kind of situations, that there are many worried parents out there. They have a son or daughter they know is in trouble, but they have no clue where they are or what's really going on.

There has been much healing and restoration with my family since this all started. I was blessed with wonderful parents and a supportive family. I wanted to take this chance to offer hope to those parents who might have picked up this book because their child or loved one is missing from the family at the moment. With that thought in mind, I asked my mother, Shelli Baggett, if she would share some of her heart, detailing some of her journey through the over two years when she did not know where I was or what I was doing. She graciously said she would be glad to share.

So parents, grandparents, loved ones who are waiting for someone to return to you, listen closely to what my mother has to say. Take her words to heart. It is our prayer together that her experiences will be a beacon of hope and faith for you. With great love and thanks to God for her and my dad, Bob Oaks, I give you my mom, Shelli.

For I am confident of this very thing, that He who began a good work in you will perfect it until the day of Christ Jesus. And this I pray, that your love may abound still more and more in real knowledge and all discernment, so that you may approve the things that are excellent, in order to be sincere and blameless until the day of Christ; having been filled with the fruit of righteousness which comes through Jesus Christ, to the glory and praise of God.

Philippians 1:6, 9-11, NASB

When I was young, before I even married, I had these verses and so much more in my heart. My deepest desire was to be married with children and have "heaven in my home." I actually had a mini-vision way back. In the vision, I had two children, a girl and a boy. The girl was older than her brother. I saw them getting off the school bus together, swinging their books, carrying their lunch pails and walking home in front of several houses on our street. It was a picture of Heaven on earth with Mommy and Daddy and plenty of food and provision all around.

When our children came, indeed, we did have our little girl, Kylie, first. Her little brother, Cody, followed. For me, loving those children was part of that love process from God. I loved them so much. I knew that one day I would stand before the Lord and give an account of what I had done in the flesh here on earth. Jesus will be handing out rewards to those of us who are Christians, and I knew I would one day be rewarded for how I raised my children.

Let's move forward in time to a certain Christmas Day morning. By this time, Kylie's brother was in flight school in Kansas City. He was staying with friends because the weather was bad and he couldn't get home for Christmas. And at the same time, Bob and I didn't know where Kylie was. We didn't know if she was dead or alive.

That morning I thought I was getting up early, but Bob beat me to it. I pulled on my bathrobe and walked into the family room to find him sitting there on his stool, quiet, eyes closed. I moved over to him and put my arms around him from behind. He had been crying and had big tears in his eyes. His anguish filled the room. In that moment, he said through his crying, "Shelli, where did we go wrong? It's Christmas morning, and our family is gone."

I stood there with my heart breaking as well, but I knew that I had to be strong in the moment. We couldn't both be weak at the same time. It was my time to be strong. So trying to lighten the atmosphere a little I said to him, "You still have me. What about me?"

Later on in the morning, I was reading my Bible when the enemy came against me and tried to tell me that I should have done this or that thing differently. I knew that was the accuser of the brethren speaking, and I knew I could overcome him by the Word and the blood. I needed to get into the Word more, so I began getting up early every morning to feed on the Word and read it to the devil.

During the time when I didn't know where Kylie was, I would say, "Worry, in the name of Jesus, get off of me." The not knowing was so hard. My mind would want to run away to bad thoughts, to fearful thoughts. I had to talk to myself and to the devil constantly.

One of those early mornings, Bob woke up and found me missing from the bed. He came to me and said, "Shelli, every morning I wake up and see that you're up at two or three in the morning. And here you are. You're not sleeping. I might be losing my daughter, but I am not losing my wife at the same time. You get over this and find victory and get back into this bed."

That was a real moment of discovery for me. It was a turning point in my walk through the situation. Satan would like to pull you in all different directions and take you out with the pain and grief. I had to shake myself up out of the self-pity and guilt of the past and get on the victory side. I love the Word of God. It's the shelter of my life. It's what I know is the answer.

> **Therefore whosoever heareth these sayings of mine, and doeth them, I will liken him unto a wise man, which built his house upon a rock: And the rain descended, and the floods came, and the winds blew, and beat upon that house; and it fell not: for it was founded upon a rock. And every one that heareth these sayings of mine, and doeth them not, shall be likened unto a foolish man, which built his house upon the sand: And the rain descended, and the floods came, and the winds blew, and beat upon that house, and it fell: and great was the fall of it.**
>
> **Matthew 7:24-27**

I knew that it was the house built on the rock that makes it, the person who both hears the Word and does it. I knew all this when I was going through this time and it was an invaluable help to us. We were parents who knew to do the Word of God. We knew to practice it and not just preach it from the pulpit.

You have to do it. Read it. Meditate it. Confess it. Over and over. Faith comes by hearing and hearing that Word!

Bob and I had a lot to deal with in all this, both individually and as a couple. We each were dealing with so much emotion and fear and guilt. The battle was constant, but every time we would stand on the Word and battle through it, peace would come again. It was a daily effort, sometimes moment-to-moment, breath-to-breath, it seemed.

The Lord led us to look at the instructions given to Joshua concerning the walls of Jericho (Joshua 6). The people were told to circle the city a certain number of times, then shout on the last day. Anyone can shout when the walls are down, but the people that day shouted when the walls were still up. It was a shout of faith, a shout of victory!

Right after Bob told me that he wasn't losing his wife and that I wasn't going down with Kylie, we were invited to a church service in Houston, Texas. We walked into this large church, and God was the keynote speaker that evening! The praise and worship was wonderful. We were doing a victory song that said, "I will dance and I will run ...."

A church of a thousand people, by the unction of the Holy Spirit, began to run. I looked at Bob and said, "I'm shouting! This is my shout of victory for Kylie. We may not know if she is dead or alive, but by faith in the name of Jesus, I know Jesus is delivering her out of trouble." We looked at each other, and by the strength of the Holy Spirit, I began to run around that church. Supernatural joy, strength, and knowing that God the Father had Kylie and everything was fine, took over me. I felt like the weight of the world had lifted from my shoulders!

A few weeks after that, I got a phone call from my mother. I heard her say, "You might want to come over (to Prayer Mountain)." Kylie was there! Bob and I went out to the first prayer cabin. We walked in to find our daughter ranting and raving. She couldn't sit still. I knew it was demons. She was uncomfortable. We couldn't pray for her. We could do nothing.

Bob and I went into the kitchen. He said, "What are we going to do?" We prayed, *Lord, You know what to do. Show us what to do and we will do it. Anything.* Suddenly God showed us what to do! We found a great big bowl and filled it with warm water, got towels, and then we rejoined Kylie in the living room.

Kylie was sitting in a chair. Without either of us saying a word, we began to wash her feet and love her silently. The love of God! We didn't have any sermon. There was nothing to say; it was ministry. It was the love of God and the anointing of the Holy Spirit that began to heal her. She never turned back. It was about a year before she came home.

The winds, floods, and rains come to every house. If they have come to your house, to your family, know that the love of God never fails. The same Word of God and love of God that worked in my daughter to bring healing and wholeness to her is the same Word of God and love of God that sustained her father and me as we walked it out from our place. What He did for us, He will do for you!

About the Author

Kylie, a graduate of Rhema Bible Training Center, also holds a degree in Television Production and advance certifications in Christian counseling. She is a strongly anointed singer and musician, and uses the vehicle of praise and worship to lead people into the presence of the Lord. It is her desire to see the body of Christ rise up and walk in the Truth of God's Word. She and her husband, Jimmy, live in northwestern Arkansas, with their daughters.

PRAYER OF SALVATION

God loves you — no matter who you are, no matter what your past. God loves you so much that He gave His one and only begotten Son for you. The Bible tells us that "...whoever believes in Him shall not perish but have eternal life" (John 3:16 NIV). Jesus laid down His life and rose again so that we could spend eternity with Him in heaven and experience His absolute best on earth. If you would like to receive Jesus into your life, say the following prayer out loud and mean it from your heart.

Heavenly Father, I come to You admitting that I am a sinner. Right now, I choose to turn away from sin, and I ask You to cleanse me of all unrighteousness. I believe that Your Son, Jesus, died on the cross to take away my sins. I also believe that He rose again from the dead so that I might be forgiven of my sins and made righteous through faith in Him. I call upon the name of Jesus Christ to be the Savior and Lord of my life. Jesus, I choose to follow You and ask that You fill me with the power of the Holy Spirit. I declare that right now I am a child of God. I am free from sin and full of the righteousness of God. I am saved in Jesus' name. Amen.

If you prayed this prayer to receive Jesus Christ as your Savior for the first time, please contact us on the Web at **www.harrisonhouse.com** to receive a free book.

Or you may write to us at

Harrison House • P.O. Box 35035 • Tulsa, Oklahoma 74153

The Harrison House Vision

Proclaiming the truth and the power
Of the Gospel of Jesus Christ
With excellence;

Challenging Christians to
Live victoriously,
Grow spiritually,
Know God intimately.

www.ingramcontent.com/pod-product-compliance
Lightning Source LLC
Chambersburg PA
CBHW070827100426
42813CB00003B/518